Poverty and Politics

The Inside Story of the CPAG Campaigns in the 1970s

Poverty and Politics

The Inside Story of the CPAG Campaigns in the 1970s

Frank Field

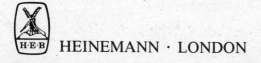

HEINEMANN · LONDON

Heinemann Educational Books Ltd
22 Bedford Square, London WC1B 3HH
LONDON EDINBURGH MELBOURNE AUCKLAND
HONG KONG SINGAPORE KUALA LUMPUR NEW DELHI
IBADAN NAIROBI JOHANNESBURG
EXETER(NH) KINGSTON PORT OF SPAIN

First published 1982

British Library Cataloguing in Publication Data

Field, Frank
Poverty and politics.
1. Child Poverty Action Group—History
I. Title
362.8′282′0941 HV685.G7

ISBN 0-435-82305-1
ISBN 0-435-82306-X Pbk

Phototypesetting by Georgia Origination, Liverpool
Printed in Great Britain by Biddles Ltd, Guildford, Surrey

Contents

Preface

Poverty and Politics: the Inside Story of the CPAG Campaigns during the 1970s traces the poverty campaigns of the 1970s. Much of the Child Poverty Action Group's policy and much of the ammunition for its campaigns was drawn from the essays which form the second half of this volume. Most of this material was given in lectures to university audiences and is reproduced here, largely in its original form, as part of a documentary record of the campaigns. Hence statistical and other information included relates to the time of writing unless otherwise stated.

Inevitably, when essays written at different times and intended to stand in their own right are brought together, there will be some overlapping material. This has been kept to a minimum, but it would not have been possible to edit out all repetition without, in some cases, doing an injustice to the original.

The first half of this volume has been newly written and tries to give both a background to CPAG's campaigns as well as a detailed exposition of the Group's strategy and lobbying techniques. In one or two places, however, I have not been able to give specific dates and places for important events. The reason for this is that after the leak of Cabinet papers on child benefits I burned substantial parts of my diaries. I feared that the the Special Branch might have tried to piece together from the meetings recorded over a number of years the likely source of the Cabinet minutes. Likewise, some of the dates in 'Killing a Commitment' are wrong. I burned all the papers after writing the *New Society* article. I then noticed that some of the dates for Cabinet meetings did not correspond to the normal Tuesday and Thursday cycle of gatherings at No. 10 Downing Street. I thought I must have dictated the wrong dates in writing the article and altered them to the nearest Tuesday or Thursday of the appropriate week. In his statement to the House the Prime Minister noted what he called 'textual errors' and this unintentionally led the Special Branch down a number of blind alleys.

Malcolm Wicks kindly commented on the text. Kay Macleod also read through the draft and gave detailed comments on both its style and content. My secretary, Joan Hammell, fitted in preparing the manuscript for press while covering much other work as well and Michael March kindly edited the finished product. I am grateful to all four for their help.

Frank Field
Birkenhead
October 1981

Acknowledgements

The author and the publishers wish to thank the following for kind permission to reproduce the author's material which they originally published (the numbers in brackets give the page numbers in this book on which the material appears): New Society (108–13), David Piachaud and the New Statesman (104–7); Oxford University Press (162–75).

None of these authors or publishers have of course any responsibility for this volume.

List of Tables

PART I

Pressure Group Politics

Introduction

The words 'child allowances' hardly conjure up a picture of revolution. Yet within the campaigns to establish and develop an adequate system of family allowances or child benefits are the seeds of revolution. The demand that the living standards of working families should not be determined solely by the size of the bread-winners' earnings amounts to nothing less than a full frontal attack on the centuries-old view that work should be the sole or prime factor. The payment of family allowances as of right, and financed from taxation, was also a major break from the insurance principle which underlies the non-means-tested welfare state. Moreover, the campaign for child benefits has major implications for the structure of British politics, cutting across class interests and mounting an attack on the class mould of twentieth-century British politics. Not surprisingly, the campaign for family allowances and later child benefits has been a long, and often heated, struggle.

In 1945, after decades of agitation, family allowances for each child except the first were finally conceded. Thirty years later, after a protracted political struggle, further concessions were made and the child benefit scheme was introduced. This collection of essays examines various aspects of the campaigns which were necessary to bring about this revolution. More specifically, their constant theme is how the campaign initiated by Eleanor Rathbone in 1918 was continued by the Child Poverty Action Group from 1965. The main emphasis of the volume is an analysis of the anti-poverty campaigns launched by CPAG during the ten years I was responsible for the Group. The volume falls into two parts. The second consists of those papers which were of crucial importance to the ten years of pressure group campaigning and, in particular, the movement from a poverty to a family lobby. Part 1: Pressure Group Politics is an essay that sets the scene for those papers by examining the political pressures lined up, sometimes for, but mostly against, the changes advocated by the Group.

There are, of course, dangers in recalling events from the inside, particularly when the author is not attempting to write an official history of the sixty-year long struggle for adequate child benefits or of CPAG's role in this campaign. Such an exercise can lack the necessary degree of detachment which gives a basis for judgement about the events being recalled. Against this the insider has countervailing advantages. None of the accounts published over the past few years explaining both the workings and the success of CPAG consider the dynamics of a small pressure group, and how these have a fundamental bearing on the nature, duration and effectiveness of particular campaigns.

The first half of the book features six evolutionary stages in the making of policy which, while basically chronological, illustrate the various conflicting elements that made up the overall campaign. Within these stages one can detect political themes which are important to the total picture being described. For example, part of the story is an account of the political frailty of family allowances as a radical idea without purchase on any of the political parties. There is also the complex relationship between a political manifesto, its agents and its supporters. Moreover, the fact that a pressure group can to some extent catalyse public opinion, thereby creating its own terms of reference, rather than simply responding to events, has an important bearing on the story described here.

The first chapter examines those political and institutional forces against which the campaign was forced to grapple from the early decades of this century. The lack of an obvious political base in either of the major parties, the mistakes of previous campaigns, as well as the built-in institutional checks against the campaign's success are examined. This analysis acts as a necessary backcloth for Chapter 2, which looks at the early history of CPAG and recalls its development up to the period when I joined the staff in 1969. In essence it is a record of the entry of what can best be described as a group of amateur reformers (amateur only in their approach to politics — not in terms of what they achieved) into the political arena.

The third chapter looks at the campaigns of the Group during the 1970s. The period divides neatly into three phases. The first concerns the campaign against the Wilson Government's record on poverty, centring on the charge that the 'poor had got poorer under Labour'. Then came the campaign with the Heath Government, its commitment to increase family allowances, its failure to do so, and the mobilising effect on the trade unions of the Government's spread of means-tested welfare support. The third campaign describes the struggle for the child benefit scheme.

This takes the introductory essay into its fourth chapter, which is a consideration of whether the campaigns, style, support and influence of the CPAG during this period lead to a modification of the political scientists' model of pressure-group politics. Chapter 5 attempts to draw up a balance sheet of the Group's campaign for the poor during the 1970s. It reviews the evidence of what has happened to the numbers of poor, the extra resources devoted to families with children, and particularly poor families, and the distinct change in attitudes of the poor and others towards their poverty.

The final chapter of the essay attempts to outline what might be the possible course of the next stage of the campaign in the 1980s. The introduction of child benefit lays the basis for a family lobby and, as well as outlining likely courses of action, this section examines the ideas developed in the universities and elsewhere on the horizontal distribution of income. The child benefit scheme made these ideas politically relevant and this part of the story is therefore a vignette on the relationship between the development of ideas and their translation into political action.

1 The Political Setting

Poverty and family support

As John Macnicol ably describes, the Victorian concept of 'family support' had passed, via the Poor Law Act of 1834, from a system of allowances in supplementation of reduced wages, to practices which were, by the end of the nineteenth century, based on both the 'Workhouse Test' and outdoor relief. In neither case was there any attempt to determine or provide for the family unit on a systematic or compassionate basis.(1) From the 1870s, however, politicians and businessmen became increasingly concerned about the state of national fitness, and the failure of the British effort in the Boer War, and more particularly the damning medical reports on the condition of army recruits, sparked off a major debate in this country about national efficiency, and inspired national concern about nutrition, poverty and physical fitness.(2) By the early years of this century some of the participants to this debate, particularly the Fabians, had directed the argument to the needs of children by initiating a campaign for a state scheme for the maintenance of children.

The work Seebohm Rowntree published in 1901 on the extent of poverty in York added weight to these arguments. Rowntree found that over 43 per cent of the wage-earning class and almost 28 per cent of the total population of the city were living in poverty. Rowntree's findings were also used by those campaigning for 'a living wage'. But a living wage was based on the assumption of a household comprising a husband, wife and three children. It was this central assumption that Eleanor Rathbone attacked in her classic study, *The Disinherited Family*.(3) Working during the First World War in her native city of Liverpool, Eleanor Rathbone had been converted to the idea of family allowances 'partly by the experience of the admirable effects of war-time separation allowances'(4) and, she was quick to point out, the beneficial effect on families' living standards of part of the family's income going directly to the mother. In 1918, the 1917 Committee gave birth to the Family Endowment Society headed by Eleanor Rathbone.

While there is no way of telling how long Eleanor Rathbone thought it would take to establish a system of child endowments, it is doubtful whether she would have foreseen that the campaign would still be going more than sixty years later. But behind the innocent phrase — 'child endowment' — lies a series of explosive ideas aimed at redistributing income between the sexes and between the generations. If one adds that these demands fail to fit easily into the class contours of British politics, one then has some idea of why Eleanor Rathbone and her successors have encountered so much opposition over the years.

Until recently it had been assumed that the Family Endowment Society played a major role in bringing about the family allowance system. This view has been attacked in the work of John Macnicol, who argues that the Society 'seems not to have been of crucial importance' in winning the reform. Macnicol believes that:

> In the final analysis . . . family allowances were acceptable to policy makers only for reasons of economic control: in the short term, they came into favour at the start of the Second World War as part of an anti-inflation wage control policy; in the long term, they were seen as a means of enforcing work incentives, assisting labour mobility and concealing the problem of low pay.(5)

An overall judgement on the Family Endowment Society needs to take into account the support it built up in some quarters for family allowances, and how this widened the options open to the Coalition Government. But it also needs to examine, as this essay does, the opposition aroused in major groups by the campaigning tactics of the Society. The point of recalling this hostility is that such opposition over the years has been woven into the political culture in which CPAG began campaigning in 1965.

This chapter recalls first how the earlier campaigners aroused fairly widespread opposition from within the leadership of trade unions while simultaneously failing to gain support from women's organisations. Moreover, the tactical failures of early campaigns, often emphasising the importance of family allowances as a means to increasing the birth rate, together with the research findings of the early 1950s, worked against the family allowance interest once the scheme was established. In addition, while there were institutional barriers which prevented pressure from developing in Whitehall to maintain, let alone increase, the real value of family allowances, the greatest threat to the scheme came from the agnostic response from both the major political parties, which has always left the scheme vulnerable. The chapter concludes with examples of counter-insurgency activities by politicians intent on curbing or undermining the entire scheme.

The trade unions

The traditional attitude of trade unions towards family allowances was heavily influenced by fears that any concession would reduce bargaining power and prejudice wage levels. Indeed, the failure to win over the trade union leadership in the initial stages of the campaign played an important part in souring public attitudes — and in particular left-wing attitudes — to the whole idea of family endowment. More recently, and particularly from the late 1960s, trade unions have given considerable support both the need to increase family allowances and then, when these were replaced, by emphasising the key role of child benefits. But this was not always so, and prior to the Second World War trade union objections fell under two main headings: that family allowances would not only hold down wages, but divide the working class along the lines of family responsibilities.

As on so many issues Ernest Bevin expressed the gut feeling of the majority of trade union leaders before the Second World War when he charged that the introduction of family allowances would result in the 'cutting up (of) wages'.(6) A somewhat more sophisticated stance was taken by the pre-war General Secretary of the TUC, Walter Citrine. His argument began from the premise 'that people have some idea of a standard of decency and of what is right for the workers (and) of what is reasonable and fair'.(7) From this starting point he went on to assert that if the State helped to meet family responsibilities, the public's view of what was a fair level of wages would be adjusted accordingly. In other words, family allowances would result in a fall in real wages.

These fears were not without some foundation and trade unionists were expressly able to point to the fact that child endowment had been advanced as an instrument of wage control. For example, in its 1926 report on the mining industry the Samuel Commission on the coal industry backed the idea of family allowances (limited in this case to the mining industry only) because they would introduce a higher degree of flexibility into wage bargaining procedure. Many people then (as today) believed that the way out of recession was to cut the level of real wages. The Commission's view was that the introduction of family allowances would protect the families most vulnerable from wage cuts, i.e. those with children, at only a very limited cost to the mine-owners. Although the scheme for miners' children was never introduced, the idea of using family allowances as a means of checking the growth in the wage packet did not go unnoticed in trade union circles. Nor did the way the Family Endowment Society 'subtly altered its propaganda to suit each audience'.(8) At one and the same time the Society was found to be stressing to employers the effects of family allowances on limiting wage claims, to trade unionists their effect on maintaining work-incentives, while emphasising to professional groups the value of occupational allowances as a means of encouraging births in middle-class families.

Official trade union opposition to family allowances lasted well into the Second World War. Then, those opposing family allowances could point to the area where the State had responsibility for setting wage levels and show that additional payments for children were used as a way of suppressing general wage levels. Hilary Land, in her work on the introduction of the family allowance scheme, illustrates how the payment of allowances for children during the Second World War was a crucial instrument in keeping a serviceman's pay to a minimum. Indeed, Land has argued that one force delaying the introduction of family allowances to the civilian population during the Second World War was the Coalition Government's concern to maintain at minimum cost the maximum flexibility in regard to the pay of servicemen.(9)

There was also the very real fear that family allowances would weaken both the appeal of trade unions and their ability to mobilise supporters for higher wages should the allowance become an important part of a worker's budget. The argument that family allowances would divide the working class along the lines of those with family responsibilities and those without was supported from French experience. Reporting on the French family allowance system David Glass confirmed the trade union stand on this point:

> a director of the (Family Allowance) Fund argued . . . that the payment of allowances had prevented trade unions from making use of family men for helping in their 'revolutionary' aims, [and] that the majority of family men among workers had remained outside the 'class struggle'.

TUC v *ILP*

Whereas these factors reflected the internal nature and function of trade unionism, the arguments for family allowances were further confused by pre-war rivalry between trade unions and political organisations. One of the most important industrial converts to the idea of a living wage was the Independent Labour Party. This talented group was soon converted to Eleanor Rathbone's view, which opposed a living or minimum wage pitched at a level to cover the needs of the so-called average-sized family. They also espoused the corollary of this argument whereby such a minimum wage had to be accompanied by a generous system of family support.

The ILP and their industrial supporters were clearly marked off from the traditional and majority trade union response on both these counts, and these differences stemmed from and reinforced the divisions between the radical and more traditional elements in the trade union movement. As Hilary Land has observed:

> it is clear from reading the exchanges between representatives of the ILP and leading members of the TUC, especially Walter Citrine and Milne Bailey, who were on the joint committee on the living wage, that their hostility to family allowances stemmed partly from the fact that it was part of the ILP's radical economic package of policies involving a very different relationship between the trade unions and the political wing of the Labour Party. Their proposals, and the analysis on which they were based, also implied that the orthodox role of trade unions in Britain had achieved, and could only achieve, very limited real improvement for the working class as a whole.

The ILP line that trade union action alone would not be able to gain a decent or living wage for workers, and that political support would also be required to reach this goal, 'particularly irritated' Citrine who regarded such views 'as a deep insult to trade unionism'.(11)

Not surprisingly, the TUC establishment did not agree with this line of argument, and general hostility to the ILP secured the trade union block vote against the ILP package, part of which included family allowances. Here then was opposition to the scheme based on little more than guilt by association. But no matter how irrational the basis, the opposition was genuine enough. This hostility was to last well beyond the period when the ILP was a political force to be reckoned with. Indeed Macnicol has recorded: 'In the late 1930s trade union leaders still felt vulnerable to wage reductions, and tended to regard family allowances as a means of concealing the fundamental issue of low pay'.(12) Campaigners had to wait until the trade union elite was part of the Coalition Government to see a fundamental change in this attitude.

Women's organisations

Sadly, this loss of trade union support was not countered by support from women's organisations. Indeed, initially, they shared many of the trade unions' apprehensions over the whole idea of family endowment. Just as the trade union movement had long debated the trade-off between pay and cash benefits for families, so too had the debate in the women's organisations revolved around the axis of cash or care. There were, first, the demographic and eugenic implications. From the first, family allowances formed an essential plank in eugenicist propaganda. For quite understandable reasons many of the early campaigners were suspicious of the blatant class bias of the Eugenic Society's statements on the need to encourage births amongst upper classes and decrease the birth rate amongst what the Society called 'the poorer stock'. Not without reason women's organisations viewed the need for family allowances, so forcefully presented by the eugenicists' lobby, with somewhat sceptical eyes.

Second, there was the political dimension. The early feminists were far from confident that the State would automatically act in the interests of women, particularly given their lack of political clout. Many women's organisations therefore emphasised the need to develop services which would be of direct advantage to women (e.g. maternity and welfare services), rather than the provision of cash benefits. Moreover, organisations like the Co-operative Women's Guild argued that working women

> must be given a voice in the shaping of the policy to be pursued and deciding the ideas to be instilled, otherwise there might be danger of scientific, eugenic and official views of the work overruling individual and family right.(13)

Third, there was the economic argument. Women trade unionists were concerned lest family allowances were used as a means of keeping women out of the labour market. One of the most trenchant critics, Ada Nield, expressed their views in the following terms:

> The children must be cared for, and women must care for them. But not by paying poor women to be mothers. Women must be financially independent of men. But not by paying poor women to be wives. Marriage and motherhood should not be for sale. They should be disassociated from what is for sale — domestic drudgery.

This argument was not entirely persuasive. Indeed, some of those women who supported family allowances saw it as a means of strengthening the economic position of women in the labour market. Mrs Arnott Robertson, a member of the Women's Labour League, believed that the allowance or endowment should go to the child.

> Every child should have a grant out of public funds sufficient to cover maintenance, etc. Every penny of the grant should be spent on the child . . . if the mother [is] determined to become the nurse and trainer of her children, the money would be paid to her. She might if she chose, become a nurse to the children of other women, who, although mothers, did not feel themselves especially fitted to develop the best that was in their children, and who therefore continued to work outside the home after marriage and motherhood.

Fourth, there was the social argument — the fear that family allowances would reduce the husband's sense of responsibility to the family. One active woman trade unionist, emphasising the importance of a living or minimum wage, argued that:

> Women with good cause dread everything that weakens the link between the breadwinner and his home . . . each of them knows perfectly well that the strength of her position in the home lies in the physical dependence of husband and children upon her.

The extent and persuasiveness of these forms of resistance within the women's organisations and movement to the whole idea of child endowment have been summed up best by Hilary Land's judgement that 'The majority of women's organisations, even those representing employed women, have never made family allowances one of their major preoccupations'.(14) These arguments took precedence over objective evidence in the 1930s about the numbers of poor families and the importance of channeling more income to them. The lack of united, sustained and powerful pressure from women's organisations, over the past fifty years or so, on the question of family support has had, and still has, important political repercussions, particularly as campaigning failures and research findings also helped to create a climate unfavourable to a system of cash support for families.

Campaign failures and research findings

The failure to win widespread grass-roots support within the trade unions and women's organisations helps to account for the political vulnerability of today's child benefit scheme. The scheme was made more vulnerable by the range of arguments used by prominent reformers in the final stages of the campaign to get the family allowance scheme onto the Statute Book. Furthermore, post-war research played an important part in shaping today's conceptions of poverty, which have minimised almost to the point of non-existence the extent of family poverty.

The population question

Many proponents of the family allowance scheme were prepared to use every argument, whether it was technically correct or not, providing it appeared to advance the immediate support for the scheme. The lessons for today's pressure groups on this score cannot be overemphasised. One of the most popular arguments advanced in favour of family allowances was the effect they would have in reversing the decline in the birth rate. It was an argument which Churchill used and, not to be outdone on this score, the 1942 White Paper, when listing the advantages of the system of family allowances, billed one as 'the possible influence . . . in encouraging parenthood and therefore encountering the decline in the national birth rate'.(15)

Similarly, in commenting on the House of Commons debate on the Family Allowance Bill, *The Times* recorded:

> If ordinary married couples are to be urged to enlarge their families they will expect assurances that the community will not withhold its aid from them in fulfilling their responsibilities, and that their children will not be left to grow up afflicted by overcrowding, malnutrition, and the lack of opportunities. Family allowances are one means of giving this assurance.(16)

Despite what some authorities have asserted, Eleanor Rathbone used this argument herself. In the Commons debate on the National Insurance White Paper, for example, she urged action on the family allowance front because:

> from about 1960 onwards the population will be beginning to decrease so much that in each generation, that is, about twenty-eight years, we shall lose from a fourth to a fifth of our population. That is to me a positively terrifying prospect.(17)

Moreover, in the run-up to the Coalition Government's discussion of post-war reforms, the Family Endowment Society emphasised the population arguments more assertively than ever. 'This is particularly true of Eleanor Rathbone, whose language on this point often became crudely racialist and imperialist'. In 1941 she urged the Chancellor of the need to introduce family allowances because of the declining proportion of the 'Anglo-Saxon race' to the 'yellow and coloured races'.(18)

These actions by campaigners led to a classic catch-22 situation. The pro-natalist case for a family allowance reform was a subject exercising the minds of only a very small part of the intellectual establishment. Yet the Family Endowment Campaign, started by Eleanor Rathbone, felt the necessity to respond and use the pro-natalists' arguments to a larger audience, and thereby associate in the mind of a much wider public the idea of family allowances as a way of (sometimes selectively) raising the birth rate. Yet 'Whatever the confusion surrounding the pro-natalist case for family allowances in the inter-war years, however, one thing stands out clearly: at no time did the Government pay the slightest attention to it'.(19)

Worse still, the initial impact made by linking family allowances with the population question was not countered during the parliamentary debates on the introduction of the scheme. As Sir John Walley notes, there was little parliamentary debate at all about the scheme. The reason for this was:

> Parliamentary and industrial, as well as academic, support for them [family allowances] had become so general by the time they came before Parliament in the height of the war, that they never got the popular understanding which normally comes from the political discussions of new and probably, therefore, controversial policies.(20)

In addition, the priority given to family allowances with their early introduction over the other welfare state measures boomeranged back on the scheme. Again, Sir John Walley takes up the story from here:

> The priority accorded to family allowances in the Coalition Government's post-war planning also deprived them of any effective participation in the great publicity and educational drive launched to support those parts of the programme which fell to the Attlee Government to bring in; family allowances were already being paid as the first of these measures reached the Statute Book.(21)

Arguments in favour of family allowance as a means of increasing the population have two major disadvantages. First, as Alvin Shore has shown, the introduction of family allowances, or changes in the rate of payment, cannot be shown to effect the birth rate: 'A rigorous scientific demonstration has not been provided that income maintenance will lead to a higher birth rate or that it will not'.(22) Second, to link firmly in the public mind an increase in family allowances as an important means of reversing a declining birth rate is more than counter-productive when, as happened, the public becomes almost obsessive about the question of over-population. Such a marked change in mood occurred during the 1960s and was reinforced by a mushrooming of environmental lobbies during the 1970s.

Post-war research

The campaigning failures of early reformers were compounded by the results of post-war research. Inter-war poverty research had shown a clear identification between the presence of children and the likelihood of poverty amongst working-class households. In many working-class districts almost one third of the children were found to be living in poverty, and a summary of these finds by Political and Economic Planning concluded: 'Having three or more children before the war in the working class was practically sufficient to guarantee poverty'.(23)

Seebohm Rowntree's third and final study of poverty in York studied the effect on the numbers of poor of introducing the Coalition Government's and the Attlee Administration's welfare state measures. Two conclusions are important for our study. In the first place Rowntree's research purported to show that poverty had been all but abolished in the post-war world. Commenting on the results, *The Times* drew attention to the 'remarkable improvement' compared with the pre-war period, adding that the introduction of the welfare state resulted in 'no less than the virtual abolition of the sheerest want'.(24)

Rowntree's second finding was that the small residual poverty problem was largely composed of old people. While the 1936 survey found that almost 43 per cent of those who were poor earned their poverty, or were in households of the poverty-wage earner, and a further 29 per cent were pushed into poverty by unemployment, the equivalent proportions were 1 per cent and 0 per cent respectively in the 1950 study. In contrast, while less than 5 per cent of the poor were over retirement age in 1936, 68 per cent of the residual group on poverty in 1950 were above the traditional retiring age.

That poverty had been reduced almost to insignificant proportions, and that residual poverty was almost exclusively confined to old people, has left a lasting impression on the public mind.

Despite all the efforts of CPAG and other pressure groups such as One Parent Families and Gingerbread, the public image is one which strongly associates poverty with old age, for which there is much public sympathy. Little sympathy is expressed about poor families and, when confronted with family poverty, the likelihood is for the electorate to view such examples of poverty in personalised terms and to 'blame the victim'.

Institutional barriers

The hostile public attitude towards poor families in general, and the family allowance scheme in particular, was not countered by either institutional pressures in Whitehall or an active and supportive base in the political parties. Sir John Walley, who was a senior civil servant in the Ministry of Pensions and National Insurance, has suggested that support for the growth of the family allowance system was hampered by the departmental responsibility for the scheme. Beveridge viewed family allowances as an important part of the nation's wages, incomes and taxation accounts. For obvious reasons the new Ministry of National Insurance was the best body to pay them, but if the allowances were to play an important part in deciding the share of the nation's income between those working and not working (the distribution of that share going to the working population according to their family responsibilities) then clearly the Treasury should have assumed direct responsibility. The failure to win over the Treasury was a costly blunder. All the post-war attacks on the scheme have originated with Treasury ministers. Moreover, by giving responsibility exclusively to the insurance ministry, the Government set the needs of children in direct competition with those of the aged, the sick and the unemployed.

More recently, an additional administrative barrier has been erected in the path of appropriate annual revaluations of family support. Up until 1980, when child tax-allowances were abolished (except for those with dependent children overseas), family support appeared in two separate budgets: family allowances in the social security budget, and child tax-allowances in the fiscal budget. While any increases in child tax-allowances reduced the revenue to the Exchequer, the change does not appear in the public expenditure accounts as did increases in family allowances. The introduction of child benefits transferred the whole system of child support into the public expenditure accounts just at a time when the size of the public expenditure budget became an issue of central political importance.

Hilary Land highlights another coutervailing administrative obstacle to the development of the family allowance scheme. The failure of the Government to fully implement the Beveridge scheme guaranteeing adequate insurance benefits resulted in the continued growth of households dependent on supplementary benefits. Each year, as the welfare rolls grew, governments could see the embarrassing consequences of their failure to guarantee everyone an adequate income free of means tests. In the absence of a family lobby there was no such pressure operating automatically in Whitehall on behalf of working families with children. Thus, the value of family support waned during much of the post-war period as cuts in living standards were made subversively and suffered silently by families.

Lack of a political base and counter political insurgency

Although no political party gave the proposal its support during the period up to the outbreak of the Second World War (except for the Liberal Party in 1939), the family allowance scheme was on the Statute Book before the end of the war. Once on the Statute Book the scheme had obvious attractions for both major political parties — the Tories viewing the family as the corner-stone of a free society, and Labour committed to an attack on poverty. Yet family allowances and child benefits have not been viewed as mainline issues for either of the political parties. The weakness of a power base in the Tory and Labour establishments has made the scheme vulnerable to attack, and there are now three known occasions when senior politicians tried to cut back on the scheme established by the Family Allowance Act.

The first occurred in early 1958 when Macmillan's Chancellor of the Exchequer, Peter (Lord) Thorneycroft, began what has since become a regular attempt to cut the size of the public expenditure budget. In one key area the Chancellor demanded an arbitrary £30 million reduction in what he described as the 'welfare' budget. Fortunately for families the Minister for Pensions and National Insurance at this time was John Boyd-Carpenter. In his recently published memoirs Lord Boyd-Carpenter recalls these events.

> Thorneycroft in his last frantic effort to keep 1958 expenditure down to the level of 1957 put a paper to the Cabinet proposing, overnight and without any consultation with me, to abolish the entitlement to Family Allowance in respect of the second child in the family. There was no right to Family Allowance in respect of the first child.(25)

The Chancellor failed to gain what he regarded as the necessary cuts in public expenditure and he resigned along with the Treasury Junior Ministers, Enoch Powell and Nigel Birch. His proposals for mutilating the family allowance scheme would 'if accepted by the Cabinet, have left me no choice but resignation' writes Lord Boyd-Carpenter, adding that he had always been 'a great believer in family allowances on their social merits . . . (and) . . . if anyone was to try to get legislation through the House of Commons to mutilate the scheme it was not going to be me'.(26) Lord Boyd-Carpenter's daughter, Sarah Hogg, works on *The Economist* and it is interesting that the most serious and sustained support for family allowances among the influential weeklies has come from this magazine over the past decade or more.

The prejudice of some leading politicians against family allowances can again be seen at work when the Wilson Government debated how best to tackle family poverty. During 1969 I went to see Margaret Herbison who had been Social Security Minister in the early years of the Wilson Government. The point of our meeting was to see if she would ask the trade unions for financial support for CPAG, but during this conversation she gave an insight into the way trade unions block policies of which they disapprove.(27)

She recalled the Cabinet discussion in 1967 when the then Chancellor of the Exchequer, James Callaghan, argued for the introduction of a means-tested income support scheme for families. The self-same scheme finally emerged in the early 1970s during the Heath Government as the Family Income Supplement, and was then ironically greeted by Richard Crossman as 'an old friend of ours. Many a person has put it up to us and said "why not do it?" '.(28)

To counter Callaghan's proposal Peggy Herbison circulated to Cabinet copies of a round robin letter from trade-unionists expressing their disapproval of any extension of means-tested support for families. The trade union movement stood squarely behind the demand for a universal increase in family allowances and the July 24, 1967 announcement of a 35p increase in family allowances in the following April was secured by way of trade union support.

However, the Government accompanied the announced increase with the statement that ways of paying for the increase would be considered in the following budget, while in the meantime it cancelled out the rise in benefit for most families by increasing the price of school dinners. Crossman notes: 'Peggy Herbison, adamantly opposed to any move towards "selectivity" in welfare benefits, resigned on July 25th'.(29)

A shameful volte-face

The third and most notorious example of a political U-turn on family support also features James Callaghan. In chapters 3, 4 and 10 the events are reviewed surrounding what *The Observer* newspaper called the most extensive leak of Cabinet papers this century. Here we need only recall the outline.

In the first of the 1974 elections Labour was pledged to extend cash help to the first child, and the October manifesto talked of a new scheme which later became known as the child benefit scheme. The Child Benefit Act reached the Statute Book in 1975, but attempts by back-benchers to write in a date for starting the scheme were overruled by the Government. While it was suggested that the scheme would begin operation in the following year, the financial pressures prevented the Government from meeting this target, and instead they introduced CHIB which was both an interim measure and a special benefit for one-parent families. The Government gave the understanding that the full scheme would come into operation a year later.

A year later the Government found itself up against the same financial restrictions, and moves were made to ditch the entire child benefit scheme. Senior trade union leaders were told that the scheme was not now welcome by back bench Labour MPs. In fact no survey had been taken of back bench opinion, but it was later found that the Whips had offered this view of their own volition. Once trade unions were informed of back bench resistance, they agreed to a postponement of the scheme. Back-benchers were then told that the trade unions were unhappy with the effect the introduction of child benefits would have on the size of pay packets — the loss of child tax-allowances transferred money from the (man's) wallet to the (woman's) purse. Cabinet was informed that both trade unionists and back-benchers were less than anxious to proceed with the reform. The whistle was blown on this U-turn when the relevant Cabinet papers were leaked (see 'Killing a Commitment' in chapter 7), and with the active backing of the unions, the TUC Labour Party Liaison Committee laid down a timetable for the phasing in of the full child benefit scheme.

The most recent example of the prejudices of politicians against schemes of family support can be seen from the decisions of the

Thatcher Government in 1979 to reduce taxation. During 1977 the Conservatives pledged to increase child benefit as part of a tax-cutting strategy. Indeed, with the abolition of child tax-allowances, the only way a chancellor can maintain horizontal tax equity between taxpayers with children and the childless is to increase child benefits while at the same time changing the personal allowances or making changes in the rates of tax.

The Tory commitment to child benefit increases was made by way of an amendment tabled by leading Conservative front bench spokesmen to a Labour Party Early Day Motion (a procedure by which MPs can express their views on almost any topic which comes into their heads). In a press notice explaining the move Patrick Jenkin stressed:

> the amendments are very significant since they spell out the Conservative Party's commitment to treat *increases and child benefits* in the same way as reductions in taxation. In this context the next Conservative Government, which is pledged to major reductions in direct taxation, would regard improvements in child benefits which are replacing child tax allowances as part of this process.(30)

The Thatcher Government reduced taxation by something over £4.5 billion in its first budget. The cuts took three forms: an increase in the personal allowances, and a three pence reduction in the standard rate of tax, together with a significant increase in the threshold for higher-rate taxes. Income tax payers with children benefited by these changes but only in the same proportion as other tax payers without family responsibilities. The only specific change favouring families with children was a modest increase in the additional child benefit given to one parent families. The total cost of this move amounted to the princely sum of £8 million. Had the tax cuts been made on a per capita basis between households with and without children, child benefit could have been increased by almost £1.60 a week.

Conclusion

The Family Endowment Society was established in order to campaign for a universal scheme for family allowances and, by 1946, these allowances were in payment to all but the first children. On the surface therefore it looks as though the Society were successful in winning acceptance for its central demand. But in its campaigns the Society focused powerful forces against the scheme, particularly in the trade unions and women's organisations. Likewise, it failed to win major support in either or both of the political parties and, in using bogus arguments in support of the scheme, associated in the public mind an increase in the birth rate with the payment of family allowances. These campaigning failures made the family allowance scheme vulnerable to political attack, and it was against this background of a public attitude ranging from the apathetic to the hostile that CPAG began its campaign.

2 Into Politics

Political activists like to speculate on the nature and extent of conspiratorial groups in British politics and most of these efforts have been directed to identifying right-wing conspiracies. Much less attention is given to the existence or otherwise of conspiracies on the left. That such conspiracies exist, and act for the public good, is not open to doubt. Indeed, the social politics of the 1960s cannot be explained without taking into account the role and influence of the more radical members of The Society of Friends. (It should be noted that the Society of Friends also has a not inconsiderable number of old-fashioned nineteenth-century Liberals as members.) Known usually by its shorthand term, the Quakers, this group has been behind the founding of many of the most active charities during the part thirty years. This section examines CPAG's Quaker roots before describing the Group's transition to a campaigning organisation. The formation of CPAG's earlier policies, their drawbacks, and their effects are also examined in the period up to 1969.

A Quaker birth

By the end of the 1950s, as Marshall records, British social policy was shifting from 'curtailment to expansion', evident *inter alia* in the political blueprints for change, more 'grandiose in conception' than anything that had gone before.(1) All aspects of social policy had, by the early 1960s, become fashionable. Social Services, hospital buildings and new universities were among the most popular targets for new investment. Coming into office after 'thirteen wasted years', promising planning, technology and social justice to redress the 'poverty standard imposed on the retired, the sick and the unemployed'(2), the first Wilson Government held out the tantalising prospect of change, predicted on growth.

It is against this background that the Quakers acted as both parent and midwife to the formation of the Child Poverty Action Group. In early 1965 the Social and Economic Affairs Committee of the Society of Friends arranged a series of meetings on the most perennial of all topics, 'current social problems'. The meeting scheduled for March 13 was to be a debate on poverty. Harriett Wilson (who was to become the Group's influential vice-chairman), in a telephone conversation with Walter Birmingham (the warden of Toynbee Hall), suggested a discussion on vagrancy. (Walter Birmingham's immediate reaction was to comment on the sight from his study window where the problem of vagrancy was all too obvious. He advised instead a meeting to consider an aspect of poverty which had thus far gained no mention in public debate — child poverty.

Were children in the 1960s being brought up in poverty? It was to this theme that Brian Abel-Smith addressed himself at that first meeting, and the handful of people present were so agitated that they arranged a follow-up meeting 'to consider what action ought to be taken to increase public awareness of poverty and to draw up a programme of action which would prevent and reveal it'. This then was the birth of the Child Poverty Action Group.

The meeting took place at Toynbee Hall which had long been the premier settlement house, and as such had played a decisive part in 'the condition to people' debate since its opening in 1885. Here then was the old order giving birth to the 1960s equivalent of what the settlement movement had been eighty years before (and a reflective account of the settlement movement, which helped shape a vital political tradition of social reform, has yet to be written).

While a new poverty lobby was forming, a parallel lobby for decent housing was also becoming prominent. The CPAG was in existence a year before Shelter and although the latter made a much greater initial public impact, CPAG's less spectacular campaigns were to have a much more decisive political influence on policy. In addition, CPAG's influence helped to reshape the work of many older established charities while at the same time encouraging the birth of similar single-issue pressure groups.(3)

Onto a campaign footing

A month later, in April 1965, the Quakers reassembled, calling themselves the Advisory Council for the Alleviation of Poverty. The Council's first action showed an immediate agreement on the political style the CPAG was later to follow: a memorandum was drawn up and presented to Government. By lobbying the minister responsible the Group made plain that one of its tasks was to influence policy. However, none of the founder members thought in terms of a long campaign. The small group of Quakers believed that political success would come quickly. Harold Wilson's commitment, typified in his statement about the 'burning desire'(4) at all levels of the Party to see the next Labour Government abolish poverty, led the Group to believe that the mere presentation of facts would lead to action. Indeed, the Group was so convinced about the swiftness with which it would gain success that almost a year elapsed before it opened a bank account and almost as long before it accepted covenanted subscriptions. If the war against poverty was going to be over quickly, why on earth did one need a bank account? And if this was true of a bank account it applied many times over to asking members to sign up a covenanted subscription for seven years (reduced in the 1980 budget to three years).

This initial attitude of CPAG is similar to the unfounded optimism which greeted war in 1914 and the belief that the troops would be home by Christmas. But, just as public opinion took no account of the mud in Flanders fields, or the high command's failure to develop a post-trench war strategy, so too did the poverty lobbyists fail to see how, similarly, their campaigns would become bogged down in interminable committees of inquiry; and how, right to the end of the 1964/70 Government's life, the Wilson Administrations would fail even to develop an effective strategy against poverty, let alone begin to implement one. Indeed, while the Group's initial belief was that the Labour Government would act swiftly once it was presented with the evidence, its early activities and its Christmas 1965 meeting with the Prime Minister does not even rate a single line mention in Wilson's own record of the period. Nor is there a single entry on poverty, or child poverty in the index.(5)

The first discussion paper to come before the Group was written by John Veit Wilson, and from it CPAG's most distinct characteristic emerged. Although 'action' had not been added to its name, the Group made clear its overriding concern with the alternative lines of *action* which would bring about an immediate increase in the poor's income. Yet an increase in family allowances, which was later to become the central part of the Group's policy and campaigns, was only one of the alternatives advocated. After further consideration, and a paper by Tony Lynes (who later became the Group's first full-time employee), the members, now calling themselves the Family Poverty Group, made their submission to Douglas Houghton, as Labour's first overseer for the social services. (The Wilson Government grouped a number of departments who were run on a day-to-day basis by individual ministers under the authority of an overseer.)

Letter to the PM

The Group did not make its public debut until nine months after the first meeting at Toynbee Hall. In late December 1965 a number of distinguished social scientists, with CPAG's first chairman, Fred Philp, signed a joint letter to the Prime Minister urging him to take immediate action on behalf of the poor. Accompanying this letter was the Group's second memorandum. The core of this paper was the Group's insistence that 'it is necessary to find a way to increase the income of the poorer families with dependent children, both when the head of the household is employed and unemployed'. Further, as the Group had outlined in its memorandum to Douglas Houghton, it believed that 'this can best be done by increasing family allowances or by making some modifications of the child tax allowance system that will benefit poor families'.

In suggesting the first alternative, the Group proposed the abolition of both child tax allowances and existing family allowances, replacing them with a tax-free payment of 50 pence per week for the first child, £1.25 for all subsequent children under 16, and £1.75 for older children undergoing full-time education. The second alternative was a development of the existing PAYE machinery so that families not fully claiming their tax allowances would receive a reverse income tax payment. Here then, were the two proposals which were to dominate the debate over the coming decade on the best ways of helping poor families. The proposal to extend the PAYE system was later taken up by Mervyn Pike as a possible measure to be introduced by the next Conservative Government.

The other innovation in the Group's memorandum, of combining the revenue from child tax allowances and family allowances and paying a single cash payment to families, was to form the compromise offered by the Heath Government on the child tax credit front, which then ended up as the Labour Party's child benefit scheme. The promise to introduce a system of child benefits was contained in the October 1974 election manifesto and was put onto the Statute Book in the following year. However, as we shall see later, the full scheme did not come into operation until after a major public row on the Government's attempt to shelve, if not scrap, the whole initiative.

The intellectual backing for these two alternatives was not the only feature of the campaign to catch the public's interest. Just before disclosing to the press its second policy document, two of the Group's members, Brian Abel-Smith and Peter Townsend, published in December 1965 *The Poor and the Poorest*. The monograph detailed that one-in-seven of the population lived on incomes below 140 per cent of the basic national assistance scale in 1960 and that two out of five of those were living in households that were primarily dependent on earnings.

A third memorandum

Neither the Group's activities, nor the publication of *The Poor and the Poorest*, evoked a positive response from the Government for another eighteen months. Indeed, by the Spring of 1967 the Government's review of social security had already lasted more than two years without apparent results. The Group therefore issued its third memorandum, which was crucial in initially shaping CPAG as a poverty rather than a family organisation.

Since the Group's 1965 meeting with the Prime Minister, the Government had been forced to take a series of savage deflationary measures. In these circumstances it was natural in 1967 for CPAG to address its message direct to the Chancellor of the Exchequer. However, the way it did this, and the solutions it posed for helping low income families 'without placing an excessive burden on the Exchequer', was crucial to the Group's initial development. In squaring the circle of how to help the poor, without costing the taxpayer too much money, the Group developed the first alternative it had put earlier before the Prime Minister. If immediate help was to be given to poor families the only action open to the Government was to increase family allowances. Specifically, the Group asked that they should not only be increased but weighted according to the age and the number of children. The cost of this proposed reform was to be kept to a minimum by 'clawing back' the universal increase in child tax allowances so that no standard rate taxpayer became worse off or better off by the change.

First successes

The Government's reaction to the proposal was muted. The poor would have to wait until the mammoth review of social security had been completed, and wait they did until July 1967 when the Government's own inquiry entitled *The Circumstances of Families* was published. Three weeks later the minister with overall responsibility, now Patrick Gordon Walker, introduced the long-awaited reforms. Family allowances were to be increased by 35p per child but, at the same time, the minister announced a 50 per cent rise in the price of school dinners and in welfare milk. This was hardly an adequate outcome of the Government's three-and-a-half year formulation of an anti-poverty strategy. Indeed, in reply to a question, the minister was forced to admit that half of those families with incomes below the official poverty line would remain there. And some families, those with one child just above the qualifying income for free school meals, were made worse off by the Government's action. Crossman notes in his diaries that because the Tory Party's reaction was a routine propaganda attack, 'we had virtually no criticism from our own backbenchers'.(6)

Although the Government had accepted the Group's first recommendation to increase family allowances, it postponed a decision on minimising the cost by making simultaneous adjustments to tax allowances. The claw-back proposal was not acted upon until after the introduction of another massive deflationary package, the appointment of a new Chancellor of the Exchequer, and the devaluation of the pound in November 1967. Indeed, it was in the wake of the devaluation, and the Government's commitment to protect the poor during this period, that they announced a further increase of 15p in the rate of family allowances. At the same time, the Government agreed to the Group's second recommendation whereby this 15p increase and the 35p increase announced in the previous year would be subjected to the claw-back arrangement. The January statement on family allowances, coming soon after the increase in the previous year, was not the beginning of a regular review of cash payments to families. Rather, the reverse was true. Families waited until 1975 before the next increase in the universal cash payments to children.

The effect of the Government's family allowance measures — inadequate as they were — was to take the steam out of the anti-poverty campaign. This initially led the Group to emphasise the importance of welfare rights campaigns as a way of offering immediate help to poor families. More significantly, the failure to win reforms for the poor by way of discreet Fabian tactics behind the scene forced the Group's Executive in 1969 to consider whether it should close down, accede to Des Wilson's take-over bid on behalf of Shelter, or build a new campaign. This argument was initiated by the resignation of Tony Lynes from his full-time position with the

Group. In early 1969, the Executive finally opted — and not without much hesitation — to appoint the Group's first director. The title was rather a grand term for an organisation with one-and-a-half full-time members of staff, but the change from secretary to director was meant to signify a change in style of the Group's work and campaigning.

Conclusion

This section has given a brief description of CPAG's entrance into politics. The Group initially held the view that the then Labour Government would quickly act against poverty once the extent and urgency of the problem had been described to them. Its failure to do so led the Group to assume a more permanent existence. As a delaying tactic, the Government initiated a number of internal enquiries on the extent of poverty and, by the middle of 1967, it announced an increase in family allowances which was only large enough to raise half of the poorest working families above the official poverty line. A further, and much more modest increase in family allowances was announced following the Government's November 1967 devaluation of the pound. While both increases were inadequate to combat the extent of family poverty, they were large enough to take much of the steam out of the political demand for changes favouring poor families. This itself had an effect on the Group which, by 1969, was considering whether it should wind up its operation completely. This option was rejected and a new phase in its campaigning life began.

3 Three Major Campaigns

In the Autumn of 1969 CPAG advertised for a director. Working for the Group held out a number of attractions for me. In the first place it would provide a direct opportunity to campaign for poor families. As I had already fought a parliamentary seat, working for CPAG had the additional advantage of building up a range of technical information and political skills which would be useful for a member of the House of Commons.

I still recall clearly the interview for the job conducted in what was then one of the Group's two rented attic offices in Macklin Street, off Drury Lane. The interview room had once been carpeted, for the carpet remained in the surrounding areas of the room but its centre had been completely worn away as had the underfelt. The interviewee's chair had been placed in the middle of this blank spot, and there I sat. On the other side of the desk ranged the then Chairman of CPAG, Fred Philp, Tony Lynes, the outgoing Secretary, and Peter Townsend.

I was asked whether I realised how important was the job for which I had applied; the inference being that working for CPAG was somehow on a par with being director of the World Bank. The staff then consisted of one part-time administrator, a part-time lawyer, a secretary and the director. While I thought the job important, and could become more so, I remember laughing and pointing to the circumstances in which I was being interviewed. The questioning then switched to whether I knew a great deal about the issues of poverty. I said that I didn't. Tony Lynes asked whether I had heard of the 'wage-stop'. I replied that I had — just.

After a further interview, when Audrey Harvey was brought in to vet me, I was offered the job. My first task was to get to know something about the intellectual debate on poverty, and above all to build up my notebooks on how Labour's policy had affected the poor.

Poor Get Poorer Under Labour: the 1970 Budget

At that time Richard Crossman was Secretary of State for Social

Services. He had been a prolific writer on the workings of parliamentary government, and indeed his diaries on the Wilson Government were to form the basis of what Crossman hoped would be a new Bagehot. In understanding the workings of the party system, Crossman maintained it was crucial to distinguish between myth and reality; what parties believed they were about was different from what parties could and did achieve once in government. Party myths were important in that they helped to mobilise supporters in the run-up to and during a general election.

Crossman had gone on to say that one way of applying maximum pressure to a party was to question its central myth in the crucial period prior to a general election. Reading the Labour Party's literature showed that one of its central myths was its being in business to abolish poverty and lessen inequality. Yet a careful glance at the record accumulating in my notebook suggested that this had not occurred. Here then, was the basis of CPAG's 'The Poor Get Poorer Under Labour' campaign.

The Lynes memorandum

CPAG had not issued a new set of demands since the increase in family allowances in 1968, although a draft memorandum prepared by Tony Lynes was in being when I joined the Group. This document began with a brief reminder to the reader about the Group's activities since it was established in early 1965. It then went on to examine the Government's record on poverty, mentioning in particular the survey on the circumstances of families, carried out by the Ministry of Social Security, which was published in 1967. It also reviewed the measures the Government took to protect the poor in the wake of the 1967 devaluation. By far the largest section of the memorandum — a third — consisted of a review of the evidence, suggesting that the supplementary benefit scale rates were an inadequate measurement of poverty. This section appeared as a complete appendix on the final version of the 1970 memorandum.

The Lynes draft concluded by way of a discussion on the means of 'meeting family needs'. It first looked at the role a minimum wage could play, together with family allowances, in tackling child poverty, and went on to argue a case for an extension of family allowances to the first child and for the total abolition of child tax allowances. The memorandum ended with the presentation of an immediate programme which accepted deferment of extending family allowances for the first child for a couple of years, while making out the case for increasing the existing rates by fifteen shillings for each eligible child. The gross cost of such a move was put at £270 million, being reduced to £135 million after taking effect of claw-back.

A new memorandum

The draft which I produced, and which began the much more overt political presentations by the Group, is reproduced in the second half of the volume (see 'An Incomes Policy for Families' in chapter 7). The political cutting edge to the memorandum was sharpened by recalling the central place in Labour Party thinking given to the attack on poverty. A search of Labour Party literature had come up with a bevy of quotes to this effect, and the most relevant were reproduced in the document.

In an attempt to prevent any Government special pleading, the memorandum gave chapter and verse showing that the Party understood about the size of the problem — seven to eight million people living in poverty — and that the next Labour Government might well come to office at times of economic difficulty. Moreover, the memorandum went on to look at the circumstances in which the Attlee Government was elected and how it successfully delivered its election manifesto. After these attempts to close any loopholes which would allow the Government to wriggle out of the charges that were to be made, the draft memorandum went on to look at the need for a wider strategy to tackle poverty — a point conceded by Labour in opposition — before examining the interim measures taken by the Wilson Administration.

The analysis then turned to a section headed 'Making the poor pay'. Four policies were singled out for special mention. First, in opposition Labour had condemned national insurance increases because of their regressive nature and the additional burden they placed on the poor. During the Wilson Government national insurance contributions had been increased by over 50 per cent. Second, the memorandum contained a brief examination of the effects of devaluation and the failure of the Government to live up to its pledge to protect the poorest from the resulting price increases. Third, attention was drawn to the considerable increase in unemployment during the Wilson years of Government and, fourth, mention was made of how incomes policies had penalised low-paid workers.

The final section looked at four ways of helping the poor. First, it emphasised the poor's rejection of means-tested help. Second, it recalled the objection Crossman himself had made to the introduction of a negative income tax. Third, it examined some of the problems of introducing a minimum wage and, while asserting the importance of a minimum wage in a total strategy to combat family poverty, suggested ways by which any effects its introduction had on employment might be mitigated. The fourth and main suggestion was for a major increase in family allowances.

Copies of the memorandum were circulated to Executive Committee members. A considerable number wrote expressing enthusiasm for the political line it pursued. In particular, Michael Meacher, who was prospective Labour candidate in Oldham, and had much to lose from a 'Poor Get Poorer Under Labour' campaign said the document should be published. Other, younger members of the Executive wrote in similar vein.

However, Peter Townsend, who was now Chairman of the Group, expressed his disquiet. Townsend's line was that the memorandum could not be published in its present form as it did not fit into CPAG's previous presentation of its case. My reply was that on joining the Group one felt very much like a political Old Mother Hubbard with a bare campaigning cupboard; I could not see a future for the Group unless it adopted a more radical political stance, and that if the memorandum were not published I would resign. At this point Peter Townsend suggested that he would look at the memorandum again and re-draft it. This he did and, under its old title of 'An Incomes Policy for Families', a new draft was completed. (The document was in fact published as a pamphlet under the title *Poverty and the Labour Government*.)

The third draft of the memorandum expanded on the introduction to Tony Lynes's first draft on the background to the Group and its work since 1965. It also kept practically the whole of the political argument of the second draft. It then went on to develop the traditional approach of the Group when making a submission to Government, by looking at what the review of social security provisions had shown, providing a more detailed examination of the social policy measures of the Government and elaborating on the policy recommendations listed in the first draft.

Meeting the minister

A meeting had been scheduled with Richard Crossman for January 27, 1970. *An Incomes Policy for Families* was not delivered to the

Department until the morning of the meeting. The reason for this was that the final draft lacked the detailed calculations showing the net effect on family incomes after increasing family allowances by fifteen shillings for each eligible child and clawing back the increase from standard rate taxpayers. No member of staff or any of the officers, so it appeared, was able to complete the illustrative examples. In desperation I persuaded Mike Reddin at the LSE to undertake the calculations and these were typed into the memorandum on the morning of the meeting. There can have been no better insight into just how complex the claw-back proposals were than this little episode. The group had campaigned since 1967 on the claw-back proposal, yet almost nobody was able to work it out in practice on simple illustrative examples. That same afternoon Peter Townsend and I met Richard Crossman in the Cabinet Office. It was my first meeting with a senior minister and I expected that the proceedings would be conducted on a serious plane. I couldn't have been more wrong.

We sat round one of those large polished tables which it would be possible to use as a shaving mirror. Crossman had with him his senior adviser, Brian Abel-Smith, together with a bevy of civil servants. Crossman began what can only be described as an extra-ordinary 'performance'. He banged the table, he shouted, and he mocked. There was an endless machine-gunning of sarcastic jokes to which the civil servants responded as if part of a medieval court.

For an hour Crossman behaved like a spoilt child unable to get his way. He played almost every trick in the book in order to keep attention to himself and away from the argument. The only action he didn't try was to swing from the chandelier, although by the end of the meeting I was sure he would have attempted this had he been convinced that this rather grand light fitting would have borne his weight.

Peter Townsend quietly argued back against this torrent of abuse. I was uncertain how to react. Having no other ministerial meetings as a guide, I began to wonder whether this was how all such meetings were conducted. In a final fray Crossman angrily demanded to know what the Group intended to do with the memorandum. I replied that its normal practice was to publish it. He said that nobody would believe what we were saying. My reply was that in this case he had nothing to worry about but that time would tell on this point.

Public reaction

The memorandum had already been sent out to the press, and accompanying it was a press release headed 'Poor Worse Off Under Labour', although a careful reading of the memorandum showed that it did not contain the evidence to support this conclusion. In the follow-up campaign the theme 'the poor get poorer' was used to head subsequent press releases. No dishonesty was intended. I saw the role of the Group's press release in terms of a personal newspaper to the media. The release's aim was to capture the attention of the reporter who would then be encouraged to read the Group's detailed presentation.

At this stage it is relevant to stress the key importance of Peter Townsend's role in the transition from the period when Tony Lynes was running the Group to the ten years during which I was responsible for its development. The 'Poor Get Poorer Under Labour' campaign was not of Townsend's making and yet it is doubtful whether the campaign would have been taken as seriously as it was without his presence as chairman of the Group.(1) No public criticisms were made by him of the way the media's interest was evoked although later he was to bear the brunt of the academic attack on what happened to the living standards of the poor under the 1964–1970 Labour Governments.(2)

As time went on, the Group was called upon to justify the charge that the poor had got *relatively* poorer under a Labour Government. Only two pieces of information in the final memorandum supported this charge. The first stated:

> Before the Government was elected in 1964 retirement pensions and other national insurance benefits had last been raised in May 1963. The weekly national insurance benefit, including retirement pensions, for a single person, is now 48 per cent higher. But average industrial earnings were already 51 per cent higher in April 1969 — the latest available figure. It is clear that all social security payments will continue to lag behind wages throughout 1970.(3)

The second piece of information relates to the supplementary benefit rates which replaced national assistance in 1966.

> Supplementary benefits were raised in late-1969 to levels approximately 50 to 51 per cent above those introduced in May 1963, but, as pointed out above, average industrial earnings had already reached that level in the first few months of the same year.

The memorandum had its intended effect. Poverty had been

moved back towards the centre of the political stage and was being discussed widely in Parliament and the media. The immediate impact on the political debate can be gauged from the letter the Prime Minister wrote to the Group on February 3rd telling them that he had arranged for CPAG to have a meeting with the Chancellor in early march. *The Sunday Times* described these events in the following terms:

> In the war for Jenkins's ear, as the Budget approaches, few pressure groups impress the Treasury with their cries for help. This year, only four deputations have penetrated the defences and seen the Chancellor himself.
>
> Three were hardy perennials: The Trades Union Congress, the Confederation of British Industry, the Scotch Whisky Association. Their meetings with Jenkins had chiefly ritual significance.
>
> But the fourth deputation — ushered into Jenkins's room at the Treasury on the afternoon of March 3 — was anything but a ritual. The importance of the Child Poverty Action Group's meeting with the Chancellor has so far remained unknown. But they reached him by an exercise in political muscle which, over the last three months, has caused controversy and bitterness inside the Labour Party and the Cabinet . . . , and may provide a bitterly-contested issue for the General Election.(4)

Government's response

That meeting with the Chancellor helped shape government policy more than the Group had dared hope. Indeed, when the budget proposals were first announced the Group damned them as a budget for the rich, but this statement had to be retracted when a more careful analysis was made of the budget's distributionary impact.

The 'Poor Get Poorer' campaign was still raging when David Ennals, Crossman's deputy, addressed CPAG's Annual Meeting in April. Ennals was at pains to stress those aspects of the 1970 budget which were aimed at combating poverty:

> Roy Jenkins's third budget concentrated in a quite unprecedented way on poverty. It was an antipoverty budget. The whole budget was deliberately geared to help people with low incomes. He could have made his major concession a reduction in the standard rate of tax — that would certainly have been the popular choice. Instead he concentrated the benefit of his concessions on the very poorest tax-payers. Very few people with earned incomes over £20 a week would benefit by more than a few shillings a week.(5)

Ennals continued his speech by making a robust and challenging defence of government policy, and in particular looking in detail at the Group's proposals to raise family allowances to thirty-five shillings including the first child, with corresponding claw-back reductions in child tax allowances. On leaving the meeting with Crossman, Brian Abel-Smith had made the point that the Group's proposals had totally ignored what had happened to the tax threshold. As a result of the 1968 claw-back arrangements the standard rate tax threshold for families had fallen appreciably. For example, whereas in 1967–8 a family with two children did not pay tax until their earnings were more than equal to the average wage, by 1969–70 the standard rate of tax was levied on earnings above 82 per cent of average earnings.

The effect on the tax threshold of the Group's previous success in promoting the idea of raising family allowances and clawing back the increase from taxpayers, had been completely overlooked in the 1970 memorandum. Indeed, I cannot recall a time either during the drafting stages of the document or in the Executive Committee when this issue was discussed. Ennals expressed the position in the following terms.

> Let us take a man with six children and let us assume that income tax was charged at pre-budget rates. This would give him tax allowances for his six children at £438 allowing for claw-back (for simplicity I am assuming that the children were all under 11 years of age). On pre-budget rates he would have had an allowance of tax-free income for himself and his wife of £375, giving him total allowances of £813. But owing to earned income relief and allowing for his taxable family allowances, he would not actually start paying tax until he earned £790. Now let us assume that family allowances are given to all children at your recommended rate of thirty five shillings a week. His wife would therefore receive a total of £546 in family allowances which would count against his tax allowances. But you are proposing that the tax allowances for children should be abolished. So instead of receiving allowances of £813, he would receive only an allowance of £375 for himself and his wife. This means that he would have to start paying tax on a joint of income of £480 — less than the £546 that his wife receives in family allowances. So before he even sets foot in the factory, he would have to pay tax on his wife's family allowances and every penny he earned in the factory would be subject to tax. Would this man ever come to understand why?

Ennals went on to argue:

> You may say that six-child families are so rare that nothing can be proved from my example. But there are, however, over 90,000 families with six or more children. But if we look at a more common family — like mine — with four children, such a family would have had to start paying tax after

> the first £2.00 of earnings. That would again involve a massive transfer of money from husband to wife but the husband would still feel that the taxman was robbing him of far too much of his hard-won earnings.(5)

Without realising it the Group was hearing for the first time the objections which were later to surface when David Ennals was Secretary of State for Social Services and a future Labour Government was trying to jettison the introduction of the child benefit scheme (although this time Ennals was fighting for the reform).

The effect

How well the charge 'the poor get poorer' stands up to an examination is still an issue which surfaces sometimes in debate. More important now is what effect the campaign had on the Government's policy to the poor, and the development of the Group's standing and influence, which were to be important in a number of political battles throughout the 1970s. In terms of the budget, the Group's campaign was more effective than CPAG at first realised. While the Government did not act on family allowances, the budget's concessions were concentrated most on low-income earners.

The campaign also strengthened the Group's position as a powerful pressure group untied by party allegiance. By launching its first major attack on a Labour Government, the Group, which was almost totally composed of left-wingers, won its independence and the right for its pronouncements to be seen as something apart from straightforward party political propaganda. Moreover, apart from its immediate criticism of current policy, the Group was attacking a much more sensitive target — the historical reputation and credibility of the Labour Government, midwife of the NHS and the welfare state, and opponent of means testing — in short, the reputation of the party that cared about the poor. It was also to win a major commitment from the Conservative Party and one which was to haunt the Heath Administration for many a long day.

The poverty trap

In late 1969 Michael Young (now Lord Young of Dartington) invited representatives of the poverty lobby to a meeting at the Institute of Community Studies. As well as CPAG there were group representatives from old-age pensioner groups, the disabled and one-parent families. Young wanted the various poverty groups to back his idea of producing an annual report on poverty. The Institute would produce the report but the groups' backing was required for funding purposes.

At a meeting early in 1970 CPAG's position was made clear in respect to this new venture. The Group had regularly produced memoranda to Government and the gathering was told that the 1970 meeting with the Chancellor would be the beginning of a regular pre-budget session with him. As the groups would have no power over the composition or style of the Institute's annual report I was unwilling, for obvious reasons, to surrender any of CPAG's advantage in this field.

Further objections were made by Help the Aged, who insisted that any presentation of a report to Government — and that was the original intention of the venture (although it turned out rather differently, as a publication produced by Temple Smith) — would have to be on an all-party basis with representations to the Government being followed by similar meetings with Opposition spokesmen. At this point CPAG's *Poverty and the Labour Government* became merged in the discussions with the annual reports which were yet to be produced. I insisted that CPAG had already begun to produce what would be an annual report and told the meeting that CPAG would try and meet the Shadow Chancellor.

Tory pledge

The meeting was arranged for March 25, 1970. This time CPAG had sent a copy of the memorandum well in advance to Iain Macleod, the Shadow Chancellor. The mid-morning meeting couldn't have been more different from that with Richard Crossman. Most of this hour-long meeting was taken up with Macleod firing questions arising from his reading of the memorandum. He sat in a high-backed chair with the memorandum resting on a coffee table before him. While his physical movements were tremendously slowed by arthritis, his ability to ask questions illustrated the best political probing mind that I have ever come across. A bevy of specific points were asked, the page references were given, and all without so much as a glance to the printed matter in front of him. One part of his questioning fell on the reasons why the Group opposed the extension of means-tested selectivity. He again returned to this issue, asking if it wasn't the best way to concentrate help on those in greatest need. Again the argument was refuted.

In a brief summing-up statement Iain Macleod gave the pledge the Group was seeking. He committed the next Conservative Government to increase family allowances, adding that this was in his opinion the most effective way of dealing with the growing problem of family poverty we had been describing to him. Stunned at his response, the Group asked Macleod to repeat his commitment. This he did in the same measured tones used in his summing-up statement.

The original aim of the Group had been to force the Labour Government into making a major increase in family allowances. When this policy looked like failing, the Group's fall-back position — and only then pursued after the original strategy had failed — was to get a commitment from the Tory Opposition before the election. It was hoped that this would act as a further lever on the Labour Government and prise from it the sought-for increase in family allowances. No such increase was forthcoming and senior Labour politicians cynically (and as it turned out, correctly) dismissed the Conservative pledge as nothing but a mere paper promise on which the Opposition would renege once in Government.

There the argument rested until it was overtaken by Harold Wilson's snap decision to call the election in early summer. Once the election campaign was underway the Conservatives made even greater play on the Group's claim about the poor being worse off under Labour. Alan Watkins, who was then the *New Statesman*'s political correspondent, went so far as to report that no meeting or rally of Edward Heath was complete without his reference to the findings of the Child Poverty Action Group. Watkins commented that the audience listened to Heath's indictment of Labour's record to the poor in bemused silence, adding that none of those present in the meeting had heard of Child Poverty Action Group and certainly very few of them believed of the existence of widespread family poverty. Nevertheless the point was being made by the Opposition leader and received sympathetically by the Conservative Party activists.

It was at this point that the Group wrote to Heath asking him to underwrite Macleod's pledge. The Conservative election manifesto read: 'We will tackle the problem of family poverty and ensure that adequate family allowances go to those families that need them'. The Group asked: 'Does this reinforce the pledge Mr Macleod has given...that a universal increase in family allowances will be accompanied by a simultaneous adjustment to tax allowances?'.(6)

In his reply the Conservative leader wrote: 'We accept that . . . the only way of tackling family poverty in the short-term is to increase family allowances and operate the claw-back principle'.(7)

Introduction of FIS

That pledge was never fulfilled by the Heath Administration. Macleod died in July 1970, and was succeeded by Anthony Barber as Chancellor of the Exchequer. In the autumn of 1970 Anthony Barber announced the Government's intention to introduce a new cash benefit for families — the Family Income Supplement.

It fell to the Social Services Secretary, Sir Keith Joseph, to defend the Government's breaking of an election pledge. In doing so, Joseph put forward three reasons why FIS was chosen and the pledge on family allowances set aside. In the first place Joseph said, he realised, 'when I came closer to the figures, that family poverty is not afflicting only families with large numbers of children'. About a third of those families where the breadwinner was working, and who were living on incomes below the supplementary benefit line, had only one child, and Joseph argued that the existing family allowance scheme would bring no help to these families. In the second place 'an increase in family allowances at the level which has been discussed, whether taxed or tax-free, could not provide the scale of help the very poorest of wage-earning households desperately need'.

The third argument put forward by the Social Services Secretary was identical to that used by Labour ministers in resisting CPAG's pre-budget demands. Once in office the Conservative Government had 'found that the scope for claw-back was much smaller than we or, I think, the whole House on both sides had realised'.(8)

The Minister's figures on the tax threshold were dramatic. In 1967 a married man with three children began paying tax at £23.00 a week. By 1970 this had fallen to £16.05, and these figures took no account of the changing value of money. Even more dramatic was the effect of the increase in revenue to the poor of any change in family allowances accompanied by claw-back. In 1968 an additional £180 million on family allowances would have directed £47 millions to the poor. By 1970, the same increase in family support would have distributed only £6 million to poor families. That these were arguments for raising the tax threshold in the budget, rather than reducing the rate of tax — and particularly the tax rates to the higher bands of tax, which is precisely what the Chancellor did — went largely unsaid and unnoticed.

The political impact of introducing FIS was fundamental and far-reaching. While the immediate embarrassment for the Government was the breaking of an election promise, the main political challenge came with the whole poverty trap debate, which still rumbles on today.

As FIS is a means-tested benefit, the value of the supplement falls as the recipient's income rises. The scheme works on a 50 per cent withdrawal or tax rate, so that that for each £1 increase in earnings 50p is subtracted from the FIS entitlement. At a certain point, originally £18 a week for a one-child family, and now £74 a week, a family ceases to be eligible for FIS. The FIS eligibility level then, as now, was above the tax threshold, with the result that a person over certain bands of income would be eligible for FIS and would pay tax. This meant that as a family's earnings increased by £1, they would not only lose 50p from FIS, but would also become eligible for tax and national insurance contributions. Thus, large numbers of poor families effectively had marginal tax rates well in excess of 80 per cent and some had effective marginal rates of tax above the top rate of surtax.

But for some families the position was even worse. As David Piachaud and I wrote in an article which coined the phrase 'the poverty trap',

> Hundreds of thousands of trade unionists are not getting what they bargained for. It is now a fact that for millions of low-paid workers very substantial pay increases have the absurd effect of increasing only marginally their family's net income and in some cases actually make the family worse off.

The article went on to assert:

> We have reached the position where it is positively detrimental to many members' interests for the general unions to negotiate large wage increases. What should trade unions be asking for in this situation?(9)

Response to the poverty trap

The poverty trap article posed the question, 'How can trade unions spring their low-paid members from the Government's poverty trap?'. The article answered this by suggesting two alternative strategies. The first 'is to try and blast the low paid out of the means-test net'. To achieve this unions would be required to win wage increases of between 40 and 50 per cent for the low paid. The other strategy outlined in the article was the less inflationary alternative of linking more-modest wage rises to substantial increases in family allowances. That this was not a message to which trade unionists were ready to respond was clear from their immediate reaction.

Jack Jones was the first senior trade union leader to answer the poverty trap argument, and his initial response is important for it shows how far the trade unions' argument moved in the months following the article's publication. In opening his reply Jack Jones conceded the importance of the poverty trap argument — and even claimed that trade unionists were already using it in wage negotiations — but went on to add:

> But to talk as if concessions in the state benefits field can be used as a *quid pro quo* for wage restraint in some form of 'annual negotiations' is to fly in the face of reality.(10)

The main gist of Jones's response was to put the emphasis on raising low wages. Jones insisted that 'Pressure to lift minimum wage levels helps to make the case against the "poverty gap", and arguments against means testing reinforce the higher wages case'. In conclusion he asserted: 'Trade unions and all people of goodwill have to work for a good social security system', adding the very important rider 'without undermining the independent organisation of workers into powerful trade unions, for this is one of the most important ingredients of a successful democracy'. On this score, as on many others, Jack Jones was as good as his word, and it was not long before the T & G, together with other unions, were pressurising publicly and powerfully for increases in family allowances. Jack Jones's and David Basnett's support was crucial a few years later in rescuing the child benefit scheme.

An even more prickly initial response came from the General and Municipal Workers' Union. Replying to a poverty trap article in *Tribune* Charles Donnett and David Lipsey commented on the effect of the poverty trap whereby wage increases might make some workers worse off. Donnett and Lipsey replied 'Perhaps they would like us to ask the employers for pay *cuts* in future — but we doubt if they will have many *Tribune* readers behind them!'.(1)

In their counter-argument Donnett and Lipsey confused means tested and universal support. They wrote:

> It would seem that Field and Piachaud see no point in removing the need for workers to rely on state benefits. Our members feel differently: they don't want to fall back on Family Income Supplement in order to keep their families. They want to be able to go home at the end of the week with a living wage in their hard-earned wage packet.

Here then was the living wage argument again, but without the basis the ILP had given to ensuring an adequate system of state support for children accompanied by a decent minimum wage. Once again the living wage was to cover an average-sized family although only a minority of workers had an average-sized family. Moreover, no distinction was made between means-tested support, which certainly is unpopular with large numbers of workers, and which is lost as income rises, and universal support, such as family allowances, and now child benefits, which are kept irrespective of the level of income.

In the event the trade unions were much quicker to grasp the poverty trap argument and use it in their favour than was the Government. Despite the Government's insistence on creating an incentive-based society, their policies after 1970 moved in the opposite direction for the low paid. The combination of inflation, low tax thresholds, the persistence of poverty wages, together with the extension of means-tested benefit all gelled together in the poverty trap argument.

Above all, the poverty trap debate was to make relevant to trade unions the argument CPAG had been putting over for a number of years by demonstrating in a practical way that they could no longer remain neutral and outside the social policy debate. If they did, then much of their action on the collective bargaining front would be wiped out by the overall impact of taxes and means-tested assistance. Thus while trade unions were soon using the poverty trap argument in wage negotiations — the miners' pay claim which ended up before the Wilberforce Committee of Inquiry is one example, and the work NUPE did in using the idea of presenting its pay claims for low-paid local authority and NHS workers is another — they also began to take much more seriously the need to get family allowances raised to a decent level.(12)

The child benefit success

Earlier, in the section on counter and political insurgency, the events surrounding the attempts by the Callaghan Government to shelve the implementation of the child benefit scheme were recalled. In the 1974 election Labour was pledged to introduce a new benefit to help families with children and this measure reached the Statute Book in 1975 as the Child Benefit Act. Attempts by back-benchers to write in a starting date failed, although it was assumed that the new scheme would be in operation in the following year.

Harold Wilson resigned in March 1976 and James Callaghan succeeded him as Prime Minister. As we saw earlier, Callaghan had opposed the increases in family allowances in 1967 and 1968. One of his first acts as Premier was to reshuffle the Cabinet, and as part of these changes Barbara Castle was sacked as Secretary of State for Social Services. In her diaries Mrs Castle records the bargaining with the Treasury prior to the resignation of Wilson over the rate at which the new child benefit should be set. She then records:

> Although when I left the Government Cabinet had been about to agree the rate at which [child benefit] would be introduced in 1977, silence fell until 25 May [1976] when David Ennals announced that the scheme had been postponed indefinitely. Instead, family allowance of £1 a week would be introduced for the first child.(13)

What made the Government change its mind? Barbara Castle accounts for the success of the campaign to implement and then win a massive increase in resources for the child benefit scheme in the following slightly egocentric terms:

> I persuaded the TUC Liaison Committee to set up a working party to argue things out. The trade union members of the working party — Alf Allen of USDAW and Terry Parry of the Fire Brigades Union — proved devoted allies of child benefit and, faced with their determination, the Government was forced to accept a compromise under which the scheme was phased in over three years. By the time the general election came child benefit had been fully introduced at a rate of £4 a week with a promise of more to come and the Government was glad to claim it as the corner-stone of its policy for the family.(14)

Under the last Labour Government the TUC/Labour Party Liaison Committee was sometimes a more important body to lobby than was the Cabinet. The Liaison Committee certainly deserves the credit for laying down the timetable during which the child benefit scheme was to come into full operation. But, as *The Castle Diaries* endlessly illustrate the battles which took place in Cabinet to hold the Government to its promises, it is generous, not to say naive of Mrs Castle to believe that the Liaison Committee's timetable would of itself ensure the full implementation of the child benefit scheme. Indeed, as events were to show, the most important and powerful members of the Government had no intention of easily conceding the demands of campaigners.

A second commitment

Those opposing the child benefit scheme had, however, been put on the défensive by the leak of the Cabinet papers dealing with the Government's attempts to postpone the scheme (the day by day account of the struggle in Cabinet and elsewhere is given in 'Killing a Commitment'). Had this leak not occurred it is more than probable that the child benefit scheme would have been postponed indefinitely.(15) Indeed, it is doubtful if the Liaison Committee would have considered the matter except for the political embarrassment resulting directly from the Cabinet leak. The Group's first major attempt to capitalise on the child benefit leak came when all the major welfare agencies and pressure groups were called together by David Ennals, then Secretary of State for Social Services, and Stan Orme, the Minister for Social Security in the Labour Government. This gathering took place in July 1977 at the Hotel Rembrandt.

David Ennals opened the meeting outlining all the measures the Government would like to take if only the pot of gold was bottomless. As it so obviously wasn't, participants were asked what in their opinion should be the Government's priorities. At such an invitation representatives from each of the organisations rose to put forward the needs of their constituents. CPAG's contribution was left until a number of delegates had spoken and the meeting was getting a little tired of nothing more than the reiteration of David Ennals's long list, albeit in slow motion. CPAG's case rested on the material in 'Penalising all Children' (chapter 9). The relative decline of families was hammered home. The priority was clear; any resources the Government had should go into developing the child benefit scheme.

The conference not only acquiesced, but underlined this demand — at least in public. One reason for this was that practically everyone felt the twinge of embarrassment over the way the Government had tried to shelve the child benefit scheme. Also, CPAG was careful to stress that any increase in child benefit should be accompanied by pension increases — an easy enough statement to make as pensions have been increased at least once a year since 1971. In addition, very few other people at the meeting had the competence to argue against the data on relative living standards. As the ministers wanted child benefit to be the priority (although it was unclear whether they had arranged the meeting with this specific thought in mind; they made no contact with the Group beforehand to 'arrange' the agenda) there was little to no resistance from the top table. This conclusion was energetically supported by David Donnison, who attended in his capacity as Chairman of the Supplementary Benefits Commission.

Under Donnison's leadership the Commission soon took up a positive stance in calling for child benefit increases, and by the end of his term of office (ironically, coinciding with the disbanding of the SBC) the SBC had developed a powerful influence.

Further government resistance

Around Christmas time 1977 the political correspondents were writing of the post-Christmas meeting arranged at Chequers where ministers were to lay down the guidelines to the 1978 budget. Crucial to these guidelines was whether the Government was going to increase child benefit. As it turned out, the decision to increase child benefits was made only a few days before the Chancellor rose to give his April budget speech. At these Chequers meetings however, the social services ministers were able to report back on the unanimous support from voluntary agencies for child benefit increases.

The Chequers meetings resulted in stalemate, the Prime Minister and Chancellor unwilling to give way over child benefits, and some other members of the Cabinet unwilling to let the issue drop. In these circumstances the more public side of the Group's campaign opened. In 'All Children Worse Off Under Labour'(16) the Government was warned that unless there were substantial increases in child benefit they would face a similar campaign to the 1970 'Poor Get Poorer Under Labour'.

As the Government gave all the signs of digging in for a long campaign it was necessary to begin mobilising trade union support. Each of the major trade union leaders was asked to sign a round robin letter to the Government which emphasised that a big child benefit increase was the number-one priority. This practically every one of them did, and the scale of trade union support played an important part in strengthening the hand of social services ministers arguing for the child benefit increase. (This is covered in more detail in the next chapter.)

Use was made at this juncture in the political struggle, as it had been in the 'Poor Get Poorer' campaign, of some of the Group's academically prestigious members. CPAG's membership was never much above 2,000 during the 1970s, but amongst this group were some of the country's most respected academics. The main points of the Group's demands — reiterating the results of the Hotel Rembrandt conference on the priority to increase child benefit —

were drafted as a letter to *The Times*, and almost all the professors of social policy were invited to sign, which they promptly did. It's surprising how susceptible left-wing politicians are to the views of the academic community in this field.

Support was also drummed up from other and, sometimes, unexpected quarters. The women's organisations, both political and social, were asked to make their opinions known, and they did so. Attempts were also made to enlist the support of the main churches. A new contact was made with one of the Roman Catholic bishops in London, Bishop Harvey, who had special responsibility for social welfare. A short brief was prepared for him, and enough copies made to be circulated at the next Bishops' Conference. As a result of this discussion, the Archbishop of Birmingham, the Conference Chairman, wrote to the Chancellor asking for major increases in child benefits.

Lobbying also took place in the Anglican Church. Peter Dixon, a member of Synod (the Church of England's parliament) tabled a private member's motion calling for a substantial increase in child benefits. Private members' motions are chosen for debate according to the number of appended signatures. It is not uncommon for motions to be on the order paper for over three years before they gain enough signatures to take them to the top of the list. The motion on child benefits headed the list in four months (Synod meets three times a year). Synod also sent a petition to the Chancellor, signed by members including many of the senior bishops — and particularly important were the signatures of those who rarely declare their hand on non-spiritual matters.

The government gives way

While the campaigns were gaining support an irate cabinet minister telephoning the Group gave away more than he realised. The tenses of his sentences told that the debate on child benefit was proving to be both long and acrimonious. It was clear that the arguments of the trade unions, the churches, the women's organisations, and the support coming from Labour back-benchers, had failed to shift the Prime Minister and the Chancellor.

One last throw was tried. The trade union and Labour Party Liaison Committee had laid down a timetable during which the child benefit scheme was to be fully implemented. Changes in child tax allowances had to be announced well in advance of the date in which the change occurred. During 1977 the Government announced a further reduction in child tax allowances. New codings were therefore devised and sent out to employers, but the power to make the change awaited the next budget. The Government's jugular was exposed.

The Group wrote to the Opposition asking for a commitment to oppose, or at least to debate on the floor of the House of Commons, the reduction in child tax allowances should the Government fail to announce child benefit increases in the budget. While giving less than 100 per cent support the Shadow Social Services Spokesman, Patrick Jenkin, suggested that this was a possibility.

Similarly, the Group made contact with Labour back-benchers seeking their support, and in this task the work of Andrew Bennett and Barbara Castle was crucial. Andrew Bennett is one of the ablest of Parliamentary tacticians and Barbara Castle had been sacked as Social Services Secretary by Callaghan. The sacking increased rather than decreased the odds of winning a major increase in child benefit. Barbara Castle was active in the TUC/Labour Party Liaison Committee and the NEC and, above all, acted as a rallying point on the back-benches. Labour Members promised to vote against the reduction of child tax allowances, if the opportunity arose, in a budget which failed to make substantial concessions on the child benefit front.

Armed with this information the Group then wrote to the General Secretary of the Inland Revenue Staff Federation, requesting him to write to the Chancellor and to tell him what would be the likely response from his staff if all the coding arrangements which had already been decided upon were overthrown by an amendment to the Finance Bill nullifying the proposed reduction in child tax allowances. Unofficially the Group learned that the union feared its members would strike, as a partial restoration of child tax allowances, and the extra work generated thereby, would make existing working pressures intolerable.

I understand that this message was relayed to the Chancellor and certain Cabinet ministers. On hearing this information, and with only a week to go before the budget statement, the Prime Minister deserted his Chancellor and suggested that he had better give the Group what they wanted. The following week the Chancellor announced the biggest ever increase in family support and defended his decision to do so at a back-bench meeting of Labour MPs that evening. Questioned as to why he had not taken actions to help the building trade, the Chancellor announced that the Government's number one priority that year was building up the child benefit scheme; that the Government had done, and in consequence there were no resources for other options such as special measures to help the construction industry.

Conclusion

This section has described the three major campaigns which occupied much of the Group's time and energy in the decade from 1969. The 'Poor Get Poorer' campaign helped establish the Group as an independent pressure group but this did not pay dividends to the poor until a decade later. The Group's personnel were overwhelmingly left-wing but, because its first major public confrontation with Government was with a Labour Administration, CPAG earned the right to be taken seriously by all political parties. Indeed, the more the then leader of the Opposition, Mr Heath, stressed the importance of the Group's the 'Poor Get Poorer' campaign's findings, the more difficult he made it to shake off CPAG when it was highly critical of his Government's record. This was evident in the barrage of criticism as the Heath Administration failed to meet its pre-election pledge to increase family allowances, substituting instead the Family Income Supplement scheme. This campaign against FIS was important, not only in getting a full-hearted commitment from the Labour Party to the family allowance scheme, but in forging effective links between the Group and the trade union movement.

During CPAG's life trade union leaders had always been willing to support CPAG's demands, but the feeling was that they never fully understood the relevance of the Group's demands. On this score the introduction of FIS changed almost everything. At one and the same time, the unions began to see the relevance of universal provisions for families and the threat which means-tested benefits held out to trade union bargaining power. It is difficult to underestimate the importance of the poverty trap argument in this respect.

These new-forged links with the trade union movement were to be crucial in the fight-back to get the Callaghan Government to implement the child benefit scheme. The Group's success here, and its effect on the size of the budget going to child benefits, which are examined more fully in chapter 5, has to be understood against the background of the Group's year-in, year-out campaigns. Contacts made and alliances forged during the previous fifteen years all played a part in the child benefit campaign success. We now turn and examine in more detail the range and style of CPAG's day-to-day campaigning.

4 Pressure Group Politics

It has been argued that publicly-staged pressure group campaigns are the last phase in a campaign, and implicitly a sign of failure. A.H. Birch has suggested that to organise a public campaign is usually 'a sign that the group has failed to secure acceptance by the appropriate government department as an effective interest'. And he goes on to observe, 'Because of this, a public campaign is often a sign of weakness rather than strength, and if this is so its chances of success are not high'.(1) The present chapter, which deals with CPAG's pressure group techniques, seeks to give an exception to this rule. True, the Group's more public stance from 1969 onwards derived not just from a belief that political campaigns should be conducted out in the open, but because the corridors of power were unchartered territory for me; as always, necessity was the mother of invention. More importantly though, the success of this strategy — in the sense that the Group, which lacked any traditional political muscle, was taken seriously by press and politicians alike — led to an increased emphasis being placed upon it. The Group's public stance was, far from a sign of weakness, a gauge of its growing success.

First, it is important to say a word about the organisational structure through which the Group conducted its campaigns. Over the period since 1969 the Group's headquarters' staff grew to a peak of four secretarial staff and seven and a half other full-time workers. All the staff were based in London, including the one person who had as part of their brief the responsibility for developing and servicing local CPAG branches. At any one time there would be, in addition, fifteen or twenty fairly active local CPAG branches around the country. Their task was to carry out a similar watch-dog function on the local authorities as the Group attempted to do on national Government.

The bulk of the work effort of the headquarters' staff went into manning the Group's Citizens' Rights Office, which took enquiries from claimants from around the country as well as providing a service for social workers. But even in this work no clear distinction can be made between 'casework' and campaigning, for much of the material for CPAG's campaigns and lobbying came directly from the CRO. Separate members of staff, including the CRO workers, were given complete responsibility for particular campaigns — from drafting the campaign document or research report right through to gaining media coverage and the lobbying of ministers and MPs.

This section looks at CPAG's key role in using the media, its links with ministers and the Prime Minister and how these were reinforced by the Group's media coverage. It also examines the range of lobbying activities with Members of Parliament, civil servants and the political parties. Moreover, in an attempt to orchestrate a ground swell of opinion in favour of family allowances or child benefit increases, lobbying took place within the trade unions and women's organisations. The Group's access to these organisations, too, was facilitated by the coverage the Group gained in the serious press.

The media campaigns

Professor Mackenzie, noting the importance of organised attempts to influence public opinion, has argued that such campaigns are not so much concerned to create a public opinion as to create an opinion about public opinion.(2) There are two main avenues open to groups wishing to create such an opinion. One is to raise issues on the floor of the House of Commons by way of Parliamentary Questions and Adjournment Debates; this is considered later in this section. The second avenue is through press coverage. Again, in Professor Mackenzie's words: 'The daily press is still held to be the best arbiter of public opinion . . . if only because circulation figures are related in some way or another to public appreciation'.(3)

Wide coverage

From 1965 onwards, CPAG had reasonably good coverage in *The Guardian*, but achieving equally good exposure in *The Times* was important as polls showed that this paper was more commonly read by Tory MPs and senior civil servants. Slowly, coverage was also extended to the *Financial Times*, and from there to the popular papers. For a considerable period of time both the *Daily Mirror* and the *Sun* gave more than fair coverage to CPAG's news stories. Where the Group's coverage was poor, and remained weak, was amongst the *Daily Mail/Daily Express* readership.

By the end of the 1970s the Group was fairly well-known among decision makers and a growing number of poorer households, but its work was largely unknown in middle-ground England. This polarisation was reinforced by CPAG's coverage on radio and television. The up-market programmes like Panorama would occasionally give the Group's campaigns consideration. There was similarly good coverage on the early-morning breakfast programmes and, most important of all, the Jimmy Young Show. A working relationship was quickly established with what was known as 'The JY Prog'. When CPAG wanted to carry out a national survey — for example, on whether free school meals were organised free of stigma — a representative of the Group would try and get onto the programme and explain the issue. In the case of free school meals, this might be the way some poor children were singled out when the dinner money was collected by being made to stand in separate queues or made to sit at different tables. A request would be made for people to get in touch with CPAG, and the survey answers written up as a report and released to the media. Sometimes the author would be invited back by Jimmy Young to comment on the findings — although such coverage was not only limited to Radio 2.

The importance of the JY programme in making contact with the millions of people who, because they are at home, are usually out of the labour force, and thereby immune to the educative process of mixing with fellow workers, is still not fully appreciated. Sensing the programme's importance, a number of senior politicians told the Group that they had sought broadcasting time on the programme largely as a result of the use CPAG had made of morning broadcasting to reach millions of listeners. The same is true of the TV programme 'After Noon Plus'.

Exploiting the media

The media coverage had a number of important dynamic consequences. As Professor Mackenzie suggests, politicians' response to the Group was increased because of the coverage it was able to obtain, which MPs took as a sign of the Group's importance. The coverage had a more immediate impact on ministers. Early on, it became very clear that while detailed and often prolonged correspondence with a department was important in trying to corner a minister, because of the size of his post not all letters were read as carefully as they should be. One way of getting the Group's correspondence onto the top of the pile and read by ministers was to ensure publicity for the letters in the media. Partly through natural interest, but also the need for protection when facing the Commons or the media itself, ministers would then request an internal briefing, thereby getting the department's attention onto the issue being raised by the Group.

Part of a lobbyist's role is to observe the habits of those he is trying to lobby, and to use this pattern of behaviour to the Group's advantage. One key group of people the Group wanted on its side were trade union leaders. On my first visit to Jack Jones I observed that his secretary's desk in the outer office was literally covered by what must have been huge post bags, so much so that the desk took on the appearance of a paper mountain. While Jack Jones, and his successor, always replied carefully to the Group, it was important to find other ways of communicating quickly with the boss of the T & G and other major unions which would by-pass the normal correspondence process.

Whenever the opportunity arose therefore, trade union leaders were asked which newspaper they read, and particualrly the one they read first thing in the morning. The vast majority said that they read *The Guardian*, often at home over breakfast. From then on occasional news stories were placed specifically with *The Guardian*, which, while good news stories in their own right, were aimed at making immediate contact with trade union leaders. This served to good effect in 1976 when the main way of telling trade union leaders on the TUC/Labour Party Liaison Committee of the Government's counter moves against child benefit was for the group to leak to *The Guardian* details of what surprise the Government was planning at that day's meeting.

Newpapers also gave invaluable information to the Group. The court page of *The Times* is essential reading for lobbying and was the first page to which I turned after reading the *Daily Mirror* and the *Sun*. Billed in the section on official gathering, would be the list of participants at government receptions, and particularly important in this respect from 1970 onwards, were the names of those invited to 10 Downing Street lunches and dinners.

Access to a Prime Minister is understandably limited. Approaches to those who the Prime Minister likes seeing, and obviously trusts, are much more easily arranged. A careful reading of the court page produced a list of those who had access to the then PM Ted Heath, and who, one then learned from other sources, were respected by him. Three women fell into this category: Dame Peggy Sheppard, Baroness Young and Baroness Elles. The Group made contact with

Diana Elles, who was also a powerful figure in the Conservative Women's Advisory Committee. Committed to family allowances, and later to child benefit, Lady Elles has played a major part in shaping the Conservative Party's universal approach to family support. I believe she was also influential in representing CPAG as a serious non-party group in Conservative circles.

Lobbying MPs

Lobbying of MPs took three forms. The first was the more general work of asking MPs to raise issues in the House of Commons. The means by which issues affecting the poor can be raised on the floor of the House are fairly numerous. MPs can put down questions for written answer or they may prefer to ask an oral question. Similarly, well-briefed members may intervene in debates to ask ministers questions at appropriate (and sometimes not so appropriate) places. The business of each day is completed by half-an-hour's Adjournment Debate initiated by back-bench MPs, and most of the topics for these debates are chosen by the Speaker by way of a ballot.

All these means were used continually by CPAG to raise the issue of poverty in the House of Commons. Indeed, the press coverage would itself lead to questions without any prompting by the Group. But the placing of Parliamentary Questions (PQs), and particularly written PQs, was an important two-way process in the Group's lobbying activities.

There was never any difficulty of getting questions tabled. This was partly because many MPs were anxious to help the Group. But there is also a certain pride amongst some MPs who compete in what can only be called the 'activity stakes'. One way of judging an MP's activity level is the league table published each session on the numbers of questions asked by Members of Parliament. It was not difficult therefore to place anything up to forty questions at one time with MPs, providing the questions were set out in a way which limited the Members' efforts to taking the questions to the Table Office (100 yards from the Central Lobby) and depositing them there.

The tabling of PQs was important in the traditional sense, in that the Government was continually under a barrage of questions about its policy to, and what was happening to, the living standards of the poor. It also played a part in informally educating MPs on questions which the Group judged to be of crucial concern to the poor. But there was a further role played by the written Parliamentary Question in pressure group politics.

CPAG as information source

One of the Group's strengths centred on providing 'the best' information. Both politicians and the media accepted that CPAG's case was well argued, and yet a careful look at the footnotes to each of the Group's memoranda will show much of the information was gathered by way of Parliamentary Questions. This was not done by plodding carefully through *Hansard* and looking for relevant data, but by asking MPs to table appropriate Questions.

When I joined the Group there was a full-time secretary, together with two part-time officers — one concerned with general administration and the other the Group's part-time lawyer. No funds at that time were received from the Government for the Group's activities, but an important hidden subsidy was the research undertaken for the Group by way of Parliamentary Questions. The Group's monitoring of Government activity was done partly by way of PQs. This material was combined with information from the Group's branches (and later from the Group's Citizens' Rights Office when it was opened) to provide the human face to CPAG's campaigns.

There were two other contact points with MPs: the drafting of suggested amendments to bills and work with the relevant backbench committees. In the early days the Group's comments on proposed legislation were of a general kind. For example, the Group would condemn or welcome a particular measure. As time went on, the Group's expertise developed in this field to the point where a detailed brief would be provided commenting on the effect of the major clauses of the bill, together with draft amendments and new clauses.

Now that I am an MP I realise more fully how important this side of the Group's work is. When the Government presents a measure to the House it has all the back-up resources of the Civil Service with which to argue its case. Opposition MPs have access to the House of Commons research facilities which are excellent in themselves, but are designed to undertake one-off pieces of work for Members of Parliament. The main burden of monitoring the Government's programme therefore falls on the personal efforts of front-bench spokesmen and MPs. The main front-bench opposition spokesmen may gain some research assistance to help them in their work, but most MPs are totally dependent on their own skills supplemented by library briefs.

In this information vacuum it is difficult to undersell the

importance of these briefs from outside bodies, and the greater the public recognition of the pressure group's expertise the more politically valuable is the brief. Not only is a body like CPAG or the Low Pay Unit quoted in the second reading of social security, education, employment and finance bills, but the most thorough use is made of their detailed briefs at the committee stage of the bills. Staff would attend the informal meetings of opposition MPs before the commencement of a bill's committee stage, and often the staff member most concerned would be present for all or part of the committee stage of the bill.

Back-bench committees

The other area of work with MPs centred on the back-bench committees. This is part of the parliamentary scene which is given little attention in the standard textbooks. Both the major political parties have a network of back-bench committees which shadow each Government department. The ones on which the poverty lobby concentrated most of its attention were the Health and Social Security, Education and Employment Back Bench Committees. On reflection, equal if not greater weight should have been given to the Treasury Back Bench Committees of both the Tory and Labour Parliamentary Parties.

Contact with the back-bench committees served as a means of briefing Members about the Group's current work and campaigns, to provide general comments on the Government's programme, as well as attempting to win support for long-term reforms favoured by the Group. When one party is in government a back-bencher of that party will chair the committee, and this procedure also applies when Labour forms the opposition. When the Conservatives are in opposition however, the chief shadow spokesman chairs the relevant back-bench committee.

These meetings, which could last up to an hour, also gave MPs a chance to weigh up the work of CPAG representatives. This was important as MPs would often have to take on trust what CPAG was saying, and were unlikely to do so unless they formed a good opinion of the Group. Likewise, Government MPs are unlikely to table or vote for major amendments to bills at CPAG's request unless they believe the issue is important and the lobby trustworthy.

Significant in this respect was CPAG's reputation for correcting any of its statements which were found to be wrong. For example, the Group issued a short brief on the numbers of poor based on the answer to a Parliamentary Question. In a subsequent edition of *Hansard* the PQ was corrected and immediately the Group put out a statement on the Press Association correcting the memo for the media as well as providing an amendment sheet for those MPs who had received the original briefing.

Lobbying the Cabinet

Cabinet ministers are made to feel important by the departmental routine and many ministers allow their time to be controlled by the Private Office. Having access to ministers at face-to-face meetings and ensuring that correspondence is answered personally are both important for a pressure group like CPAG. Media coverage helped the Group to gain access, while the meetings themselves served to increase the importance of CPAG in the eyes of the media.

The one-off story to a single newspaper could also affect the way a minister responded to the Group. Mrs Thatcher, for example, behaved as a very tough Minister of Education and was unwilling to concede meetings with delegations unless she considered them important from her point of view. This firm attitude towards controlling her own time appeared to extend to her correspondence. On one occasion the Group wrote to her as Secretary of State for Education, and received a reply from a civil servant. In response the Group placed a story in one of the diaries that Mrs Thatcher was the only minister with whom the Group had made contact who did not reply directly to the poor. Of course no minister was replying directly to the poor, but to an organisation without any authority to claim to be speaking for the poor. However, the diary story worked, and from then onwards Mrs Thatcher replied personally to CPAG letters.

The point of doing this was not that the Group felt slighted, but rather to try and make Mrs Thatcher pay personal attention to those points which the Group raised with her department. One way of ensuring (as far as it was humanly possible) that she did so was to get her to sign the correspondence back to the Group. The hope was that if ministers signed letters they also read and took an interest in the answers being drafted.

Meetings with ministers took on two main forms: some were concerned with submitting a memorandum arguing a general line of policy, others with discussing detailed aspects of government policy. Both types of meeting, and the preparation of material for them, forged an important link with civil servants. Unlike the traditional well-established pressure groups, CPAG rarely had day-to-day contact with civil servants, either on the detailed workings of legislation, or proposals for reform. Similarly, one aim of the Group's publications was to 'educate' the civil servants. The more coverage a publication gained the more likely that the minister would ask for a detailed appraisal from his civil servants. The more the civil servants were asked to respond to CPAG's work the more they became acquainted with the arguments deployed by the Group.

After the meeting with Roy Jenkins in 1970 CPAG would normally meet the Chancellor before his April budget statement. These meetings were important in arguing the general principles which the Group wished governments to adopt in formulating an anti-poverty strategy. Often such gatherings, while unsuccessful in their immediate objectives, served as a continuing public recognition of the political importance of the Group, and this was to pay long-term dividends. These meetings also gave senior civil servants a chance of evaluating the quality of CPAG's staff.

The wage-stop

Other ministerial meetings would be arranged to discuss an aspect of government policy which affected limited groups of poor people, for example the wage-stop. For years the Group had campaigned for the abolition of this rule, which was supposed to ensure that the benefit paid to unemployed families on supplementary benefit was not greater than the level of wages they obtained when following their normal occupation. Given the Poor Law tradition that people in work should be in a better financial position than those unable to work, and the low level of child support, such a rule was inevitable. Campaigning against the wage-stop (or many of the other single issues) was significant in helping to win over government support for family allowance increases.

The attack on the wage-stop was a single one. While in earlier days the Group argued against having such a rule, later campaigns were centred on whether the rule was being operated in the way the Government assured the Commons and the public that it was being operated. It was not difficult to gather together examples showing the breaking of government's directives.

Here the Group's contact with poor families was especially important. The writ laid down by Secretaries of State for Social Services at the Elephant and Castle does not always run smoothly to every local office in the country. As a defence mechanism to this, ministers were likely to accept perhaps a single example of the rules failing to operate as an isolated phenomenon. This was Sir Keith Joseph's response when arguing with him on how the wage-stop rules worked in practice. But once the Group responded by telling the Minister he could have twenty examples of maladministration within twenty-four hours, the Secretary of State became far less complacent about the working of standard guidelines.

Pressure on political parties

Commitments from political parties were won both inside and outside Parliament. One reason for spending a great deal of time preparing and then briefing opposition spokesmen for the committee stage of a bill was to get the opposition to underwrite certain reforms. For example, during the debate on the Family Income Supplement, opposition spokesmen made much of the Government's failure to fulfil its election promise to increase family allowances, and went on to stress their importance in combating family poverty. Likewise, the briefing of MPs on select committees, and the appearance before the select committees, were all geared to gaining commitments from prominent MPs sitting on the committees, although this is not what select committees are established for. An important example of lobbying behind the scenes, and before a select committee, was the activity centring on the sub-committee of the Expenditure Committee, which had the task of investigating the tax credit proposals. On this issue, as with so many others, the Group presented by far and away the most carefully argued case of any of the pressure groups.

Extra-parliamentary politics

The other form of pressure is applied to political parties outside of Westminster. The Labour and Liberal Parties, because of the greater role allotted to their rank and file, are more open to outside pressure than is the Conservative Party. The Group was active at a grass roots level in both Labour and Liberal Parties, ensuring that resolutions on family support, tax policies, and the administration of means-tested benefits, were all tabled so that some could be debated at the Party Conferences. In both parties Conference decisions play some part in deciding the shape and content of the Party's election manifesto.

The effort at party Conference was not only concerned, in the months beforehand, at ensuring that topical resolutions had been tabled at a local branch level; briefings were prepared for Conference debates and circulated free to delegates. Moreover, the Group made its presence felt at both Labour and Liberal Party conferences by establishing a welfare rights stall, or a bookstall, and arranging a major fringe meeting. This was so successful that other pressure groups have since followed the CPAG lead, so that now delegates have difficulty in deciding which particular fringe meeting they will attend at any one time during the lunch time, or after the formal proceedings of the day's debates have closed.

Meetings, telephone conversations and correspondence were conducted with the relevant researcher in each of the political parties whose brief covered taxation and social security matters. Because the Conservative Party was less open to lobbying through branches or the annual conference, more emphasis was given to the contact with the Conservative Research Department. Indeed, considering the greater influence the Conservative Research Department has on Party policy, this was clearly justified in its own right.

Again the Group's track record in attacking the Labour Government in the run-up to the 1970 election paid dividends here. Although the Group was known to be staffed by left-wingers, its reputation in trying to tell the truth, as it saw it, stood it in good stead. Relevant sections of Conservative party policy documents bear witness to the effectiveness of the Group's lobbying, together with, of course, the strength of the Research Department's then Director, Chris Patten, in developing the Conservative party's social policy within the tradition laid down by Chamberlain in the early 1930s.

The trade unions and women's organisations

The conversation with Margaret Herbison in 1969 (chapter 1) illustrates how the trade unions use their power in a negative way to shape social policy. During the 1970s the Group tried to enlist the trade unions' active support for changes favourable to the poor, rather than relying on the unions' somewhat negative power to block proposals which the Group thought harmful to poor families. Lobbying within the trade union movement developed along a number of lines. Jack Jones and the T & G were beginning to play an increasingly important role in shaping public opinion on pensions. The T & G therefore became a target area for the Group. One possibility was to join the Union. Consequently, the staff formed a branch of the T & G and invited employees of other pressure groups to become members too. It was hoped (a hope never realised) that this branch would become the epicentre for social policy developments within the T & G.

A more traditional approach with other trade unions was to build up contact with research officers. Given the pressure under which trade union leaders work, the research officers play a key role both as a means of direct access to the union boss himself and in the preparation of his speeches. From time to time the Group informally met trade union research officers to discuss those issues about which it was most concerned and for which it wanted trade union support. This support was cemented by inviting major trade unions to appear on public platforms with the Group, and the tabling of relevant resolutions in local branches of the trade unions both for their own union's annual meetings and the TUC Conference itself. Fringe meetings were arranged at the TUC Conference and similar briefings to those for the political parties were prepared for the Conference.

Trade union support was also gained by way of a round robin letter addressed to Labour Cabinets. As we saw in the previous section, this initiative was of considerable importance in winning over the uncommitted members of the Cabinet in the crucial struggles leading up to the 1978 Budget. Trade union leaders were anxious to help the Group in this way, partly because they were committed to the issues; partly because the Group commanded respect for the way it conducted its campaigns; and partly because of the coverage the Group could get in the media.

Media coverage made access to the women's organisations that much easier. The Group's insistence on acting and being seen to be a non-party political body was also important here. Fairly regular contact was kept with organisations such as the National Council of Women, as well as the women's organisations of each of the political parties, to ensure that the issue of child support was on their agendas. When the Group was trying to build up a ground swell before a budget in favour of family allowance or child benefit increases, contact with the women's organisations would be renewed and their public support sought for particular budget changes. Almost invariably this support was forthcoming.

Conclusion

Two bonds cement CPAG activists. The first is the belief that child benefit increases are the most immediately effective way of diminishing, and indeed abolishing, child poverty. The second bond arises from the way the Group approaches its work: its belief that its first moral duty is to help poor families now and not just talk about big structural changes which in the long run will usher in a new Jerusalem. But linked to giving practical help about welfare rights, providing representation at tribunals and helping to take cases into the courts, is the Group's second moral priority. This is to use the information gained in giving practical day-to-day help to the poor as part of a continuous political campaign to improve the lot of all poor people.

This chapter has looked at the range of lobby contacts made by the Group. Of key importance was the media coverage. This was crucial in building up the reputation of the Group amongst politicians — and, as coverage feeds on itself, in the media itself. The coverage was also important in making access to other groups that much more easy — trade unions, churches, women's organisations. The point of all these pressure group activities was to improve the lot of poor families. The next chapter evaluates how successful CPAG has been in this task.

5 The Balance Sheet

Macnicol concludes in his study of the Family Endowment Society that it was not of 'crucial importance' to the campaign for family allowances.(1) Does this judgement apply also to CPAG? Was the Group little more than a body of activists who convinced themselves of their own importance? Or would it be right to accept the view of many commentators that CPAG is one of the premier campaigning organisations? This chapter draws up a tentative balance sheet. Three criteria are used for judging the effectiveness of the Group's campaigns. An obvious one is to look at the number of poor households, and particularly the number of poor families, and to ask, 'Did CPAG's activities lead to a decline in the numbers of poor or, at the very least, stem the growth in the number of poor households?'

A second possibility is to consider the extra resources won for families with children. What are the detailed figures on the extra resources paid out in child support? A third way is to try and gauge the impact of the Group's activities on the opinions of the poor themselves about their own poverty, as well as a change in the attitudes of powerful groups to the problems of poverty. Is there any evidence to show that CPAG's campaigning stance has had any lasting influence on the poor themselves or, at the very least, on those groups who are in the best position to help relieve poverty?

Number of poor

Throughout this volume poverty is defined by the supplementary benefit scale rates. Each year Parliament approves the supplementary benefit scale rates by which a person's entitlement is determined, and people outside the labour market without an adequate income of their own may be eligible for supplementary benefits. Claimants usually have their rent paid in full and their final income depends on whether they qualify for the ordinary weekly scale or the long-term scale rate. All pensioners drawing benefit qualify immediately for the long-term rate whereas people below retirement age will qualify if they have been on benefit for one year and are not required to register for work (as are unemployed claimants). So immediately we see there is not one poverty line in Britain but two, and the gap between these rates has widened steadily since 1973, when the long-term rate was pitched at 10 per cent above the ordinary rate for a married couple. For a family without children the gap between the long-term and ordinary scale rate poverty line is now £9.60 a week or 25 per cent more than the ordinary rate.

For an unemployed married couple with two children both under 10 paying an average rent of £7.40 a week the supplementary benefit allowance — or poverty line income for this family — is currently (in 1981) £60.95. In individual day-to-day terms it means that a married couple must cover 'all items of normal expenditure on day to day living, apart from housing costs, including in particular:

1. food;
2. household fuel;
3. purchase, cleaning, repair and replacement of clothing and footwear;
4. normal travel costs;
5. weekly laundry costs;
6. miscellaneous household expenses such as toilet articles, cleaning materials, window cleaning and the replacement of small household goods (e.g. crockery, cutlery, cooking utensils, light bulbs);
7. leisure and amenity items such as TV licence and rental, newspapers, confectionery and tobacco',(2)

from a daily allowance of around £5.39 and are expected to keep their youngest children on £1.13 a day.

Poor drawing supplementary benefit

Taking the supplementary benefit scale rates as the measurement of poverty, what does this tell us about the numbers of poor in post-war Britain? More particularly, what has happened to the numbers and composition of the poor since the mid-1960s when the CPAG was established explicitly to campaign for a reduction in the numbers on low incomes?

While the opening of the 1948 National Assistance Act proclaims: 'the existing Poor Law shall cease to have effect', the establishment of the post-war welfare state did not abolish poverty, as the growing numbers of poor testify. In 1948 a fraction over a million households were dependent on supplementary benefits. This total jumped to 1.46 million in 1951, rising again to 1.84 million in 1961 and reaching

1.99 million in 1965 — the year in which CPAG was founded. Since then the numbers have continued to grow, rising to a peak in 1977, when the numbers had risen to 2.99 million households, and falling slightly to 2.85 million claimants in 1979.

As supplementary benefit payments cover not only the needs of the recipient, but also members of the claimant's household, it is important to look at the total number of persons dependent on supplementary benefit and not just the numbers of individual claimants drawing weekly allowances. Information on the numbers of dependants within claimants' households has only been published since 1962 and the full information is presented in Table 5.1.

Looking first at the recipient figures, Columns 2 and 3 show the number of recipients below pension age growing in relation to those over retirement age up to 1974, with a big jump in the ratio from 1975 onwards. The 1975 SBC report, discussing the fall in the numbers of retirement pensioners supported by supplementary benefit (in absolute terms from 1972 onwards and as a proportion of the total number of pensioners from 1967 onwards), suggests that this could be both the result of a growing number of pensioners with sources of income other than the retirement pension, particularly income from occupational pensions, and of improvements in 1974 in housing rebate schemes which made many pensioners better off claiming rebates than drawing supplementary benefits.(3)

The reasons for the increase in the number of recipients below pensionable age is not difficult to fathom. Since 1968 unemployed claimants drawing supplementary benefits have grown in number and as a proportion of the total numbers below retirement age drawing supplementary benefit. In 1968, 28 per cent of claimants below pension age receiving SB were unemployed. By 1979 this figure had risen to 50 per cent. Likewise, the number of one parent families is growing at about 6 per cent a year, and 60 per cent of one parent families are dependent on supplementary benefits.

When the figures of the total number provided for by supplementary benefit payments are considered (presented in brackets in the table) the number of non-OAP recipients and their dependants shows the same jump in relation to pensioners and their dependants in 1975, and from 1975 has exceeded pensioners plus dependants. In 1974, 2,140,000 pensioners were dependent on supplementary benefits compared with 1,950,000 claimants and their families below retirement age. A year later these numbers had more than been reversed. Pensioners and their dependants amounted to

Table 5.1 Recipients of and total number of persons provided for by regular weekly supplementary benefit payments (GB)

Year (c)	*All Supplementary benefits* (1) *Thousands*	*Supplementary Pensions* (2) *Thousands*	*Supplementary Allowances* (3) *Thousands*	*Col (3) as % Col (2)* (4) %
1962	2,040 (3,010)	1,390 (1,620)	650 (1,380)	47 (85)
1963	1,990 (2,930)	1,350 (1,570)	640 (1,360)	47 (87)
1964	1,980 (2,790)	1,400 (1,620)	580 (1,170)	41 (72)
1965	2,010 (2,850) (d)	1,430 (1,660)	580 (1,190)	41 (72)
1966	2,490 (n.a)	1,820 (n.a)	680 (n.a)	37 (n.a)
1967	2,560 (3,850)	1,810 (2,160)	750 (1,690)	41 (78)
1968	2,640 (3,990)	1,860 (2,220)	780 (1,770)	42 (80)
1969	2,690 (4,100)	1,870 (2,260)	810 (1,840)	43 (81)
1970	2,740 (4,170)	1,900 (2,300)	840 (1,870)	44 (81)
1971	2,910 (4,560)	1,920 (2,310)	990 (2,250)	52 (97)
1972	2,910 (4,560)	1,910 (2,290)	1,000 (2,270)	52 (99)
1973	2,680 (4,020)	1,840 (2,200)	830 (1,820)	45 (83)
1974	2,680 (4,090)	1,810 (2,140)	870 (1,950)	48 (91)
1975	2,790 (4,430)	1,680 (1,960)	1,110 (2,470)	66 (126)
1976 (a)	2,940 (4,720)	1,690 (1,980)	1,250 (2,740)	74 (138)
1977 (b)	2,990 (4,760)	1,740 (2,030)	1,250 (2,720)	72 (134)
1978	2,930 (4,600)	1,740 (2,040)	1,190 (2,560)	68 (125)
1979	2,850 (4,370)	1,720 (2,050)	1,130 (2,320)	66 (113)

Source: DHSS

Notes: (n.a.) Not published

(a) Estimated figure due to industrial action.

(b) Change in method of estimation: before 1976 figures are based on the 100 per count but from November 1977 they are based on rating up factors for local offices derived from the 1 in 50 sample of supplementary allowance recipients and the 1 in 200 sample of supplementary pensioners.

(c) On a day in December or November.

(d) Figures in brackets relate to the number of dependants.

1,960,000 while those under retirement age dependent on supplementary benefit had risen to 2,470,000.

Part of this increase is accounted for by the rise in the numbers of children living in supplementary benefit households. In 1967, 688,000 children were living in households where the breadwinner was drawing supplementary benefits. This total jumped to 944,000 in 1971, rising again in 1976 to 1,136,000. Since then there has been a small decline, down to 1,118,000 in 1977, 1,043,000 in 1978 and 918,000 in 1979.

Living below the poverty line

For several reasons the number of supplementary benefit recipients is an inaccurate measure of the numbers in poverty. It does not, for example, include the poor who are living on incomes below the supplementary benefit level. The working poor are excluded from benefit, and other poor people, while appearing eligible for benefit, do not claim.

Since 1972, official data have been released on the number of families living on incomes below the supplementary benefit poverty line. Table 5.2 reproduces data on the number of households with children living below the poverty line. It shows a growth in the number of the very poorest up to 1976 and a slight fall in the following year. The complete FES data also show that the fall in the number of the very poorest with children (14.2 per cent) is greater than that for all persons below pensionable age (9.5 per cent) or the reduction in the number of persons living below the supplementary benefit poverty line (12.6 per cent). Even so, over three quarters of a million people are shown to be living on incomes *below* the official state poverty line.

These figures, which show a slight decline in the number of families living on incomes below the supplementary benefit level, underestimate the effect of the transition to a child benefit scheme. Most of the additional increases in funds to the scheme were injected after 1977 — which is the latest date for which we have figures on the numbers of poor below the supplementary benefit level. Even so, CPAG's campaigning has had little effect on the overall numbers of poor. The massive increase in unemployment over this period, up from 299,000 in mid-1965 to 1,334,000 in mid-1979, together with major demographic changes, increasing the number of single parent families, was bound to lead to a growing number of poor children. But while the Group's efforts were overwhelmed by these two power-

Table 5.2 Families with incomes below supplementary benefit level, 1972–1977

	(excluding Supplementary Benefit recipients) (thousands)					
	Married couples with children		*Single Persons with children (a)*		*Total*	
	Families	*Persons*	*Families*	*Persons*	*Families*	*Persons*
December						
1972	70	320	20	80	90	400
1973	60	280	40	140	100	320
1974 (b)	90	390	20	70	110	460
1975	130	570	50	150	180	720
1976	190	820	30	90	220	910
1977	160	670	40	110	200	780

Sources: Social Security Statistics: 1976–1978 Table 47.07. *Social Trends:* No. 6 and No. 7 Table 5.31. DHSS.

Notes: (a) Subject to very considerable statistical error in most years.

(b) Estimates for years before 1974 are not comparable with those for later years because it was assumed in the earlier years that the income of the self-employed was the same as for other employees. From 1974 self-employed records have been analysed.

ful forces, a rather different picture emerges if we examine the shift in resources to the poor brought about largely as a result of the Group's campaigns.

Shifting resources to the poor

Central to the Group's campaigns has been the introduction of an adequate system of child support, and from the mid-1970s onwards this had crystallised around the demands for a generous system of child benefit. We saw earlier how the Labour Party's 1974 election manifestoes committed a future Labour Government to introduce such a scheme, and the difficulties that governments had in keeping their promises.

The proposals on child benefit reached the Statute Book in 1975. Before examining the changes brought about in the size of child benefit payments it is important to recall the level of family allowance support since it was first paid, in August 1946, at 25p for all children except the first. The allowance was increased on only four occasions in the period up to 1968, when the benefit stood at 90p for second children and £1 for third and subsequent children. No changes in the rates of benefit were made thereafter until 1975 when the allowance was raised to £1.50 a child. In 1977 the benefit was given at £1 for all first children, and raised to £2.30 for *all* children in April 1978, to £3.00 in November 1978, and to £4.00 in April 1979.

In calculating the extra resources going to families with children it is necessary to reach a net figure which takes into account not only the additional benefit payments but also the loss of child tax allowances which occurred at the same time. This information is presented in Table 5.3, which looks at the various elements of family support in the years from 1974 to 1975 in 1979 survey prices. Column 4 lists the totals for family allowance, child interim benefit, child benefit, and the net value of child allowances (i.e. after deductions have been made for the claw-back of tax from family allowances and child interim benefit) in the relevant years. Column 5 and 6 show changes in the level of expenditure compared with 1974–5. Column 5 gives figures in respect of each year, and Column 6 the cumulative total. Columns 7 and 8 present similar figures but start from a 1977–8 expenditure base. Because of the fall in the level of real expenditure between 1976–7 and 1977–8 the cumulative total in Column 8 reaches a higher level than that in Column 6. Columns 7 and 8 show the effect of the leak of the Cabinet papers on child benefit and the campaign to secure a full child benefit scheme. By

Table 5.3 Family Support in the UK

(£ million at 1979 Survey Prices)

	(1) Family allowances including child interim benefit	*(2) Child benefit*	*(3) Child tax allowances*	*(4) (1)+(2) +3*	*(5) Excess over 1974–5 level*	*(6) Cumulative total of (5)*	*(7) Excess over 1977–8 level*	*(8) Cumulative total of (7)*
1974–5	701		1,600	2,301	—	—		
1975–6	870		1,600	2,470	169	169		
1976–7	773		1,700	2.473	172	341		
1977–8		1,088	1,100	2,188	– 113	228	—	—
1978–9		2,074	600	2,674	373	601	486	486
1979–80		2,820		2,820	519	1,120	632	1,118
1980–81 (estimated)		2,585		2,585	284	1,404	397	1,515
			TOTALS	17,511	1,404		1,515	

Source: The Governments Expenditure Plans 1980–1 to 1983–4. Cmnd 7841, pages 110–11.
Notes: (a) Aggregate net value taking account of the claw-back of tax on family allowance and child interim benefit.

1979–80 it had resulted in an additional £1.5 billion going to families with children. This extra sum will be paid each year as part of the child benefit scheme expenditure.

The size of this success does not give grounds for complacency. No doubt when the figures are published we will find that the numbers of poor families dependent on means-tested assistance grew over the same period during which the child benefit scheme had a major injection of funds. Similarly, this injection, though large in comparison with previous increases in support, is small compared with the size of total personal incomes. When the relevant data are published, it is doubtful whether the additional resources to the child benefit scheme will make any difference to the overall distribution of personal incomes. During the post-war period the share going to the poorest households has remained remarkably stable and this is true whether one looks at income before or after tax.(4)

Changing attitudes

While CPAG has played a part in winning significant extra resources for child support in this country, so too has it had a crucial impact on the importance of major groups in this country in any way involved with the problems of poverty. Some of CPAG's work to this end within the political parties was described in the previous section. But more important in the long run than the extra resources and the change in the views of the political elite, has been the role of the Group in helping to effect a change in the attitude of the poor themselves to their poverty.

In the middle of 1976 the EEC carried out a survey on people's attitudes to poverty. The poll was conducted in each of the nine member states and showed, amongst the community as a whole, that 16 per cent of the population believed people were poor because they were unlucky, while a further 25 per cent attributed poverty to personal laziness or lack of willpower. Twenty-six per cent of those polled attributed poverty to the injustices in our society while a further 14 per cent viewed it as a by-product and inevitable part of modern progress.(5)

The results of the UK poll, however, were at considerable variance with the overall EEC findings on the causes of poverty. In Italy and France the most common response was to put the blame at society's door. But in Britain 45 per cent of the respondents saw the causes of poverty in the laziness of the poor themselves, 42 per cent believed it was because the poor had failed to gain work, and a further 40 per cent thought it was due to the drinking habits of poor people.(6)

Any change in attitude by the poor themselves therefore has to be viewed against this hostile background where large sections, if not the majority of the community, see poverty in personal terms with a tendency to 'blame the victim'. Given the public's hostility to the poor as a mass, the early days of CPAG were characterised by the Group acting as a spokesman for the poor. Of course this role continues, but as time went on poor families increasingly wanted to be involved in the campaign against poverty themselves. The Group's central thrust insisted that poverty was caused mainly by the distribution of income and resources within the society, and to a much lesser extent by the poor themselves. As the seventies progressed, more and more newspapers, radio and television programmes turned to poor families themselves to explain to the public what it was like to be poor, rather than have a member of the Group speak on their behalf. This change in attitude — which has to some extent been reversed by the outpourings of abuse about 'social security scroungers' — stands as one of the Group's major successes.

Conclusion

It would be wrong to claim that the additional £1.5 billion paid each year in child benefit as a result of the 1976–78 campaigns is exclusively due to the lobbying success of CPAG. The battle Stan Orme and David Ennals fought in Cabinet, the support of all the major trade unions, and the public statements of support from the churches and the major women's organisations, all played a part. But so too did CPAG's expertise in spotting that the 1978 child tax allowance changes had been set in hand in 1977, thereby exposing the 1978 budget's jugular to attack, not least from the Opposition and Government back-benchers.

The reaction of the Prime Minister and his Chancellor were much affected by the lack of an overall parliamentary majority and CPAG's known ruthlessness for seeing a campaign through to its conclusion. Indeed, ministers asked the Group whether this was a re-run of the 1970 campaign. Moreover, the reaction of top trade unionists and politicians was shaped in no small way by the 1976 leak of Cabinet papers on child benefits. Such an unexpected bonus was a major factor in explaining the success of a small pressure group which lacked any traditional political muscle.

Similarly, the Group's campaigns have helped to bring about a marked change in attitudes of politicians, which itself made the implementation of the child benefit scheme that much easier to obtain. But most important of all have been CPAG's efforts in changing the attitudes of the poor themselves. Slowly, more and more poor people are seeing their poverty less as a sign of personal failure, and more as a result of the actions of governments and an electorate which supports those governments. As unemployment mounts, and this is clearly seen as a result of government action, this change in attitude and response to poverty will start to be registered in the political arena. A second decisive shift in the balance of power could take place through the creation of an effective family lobby. The basis of such a move is examined in the next chapter.

6 Next Moves

Although in some quarters implicit criticism had been made of CPAG's claw-back proposals having the unintentional effect of dividing the interests of rich and poor families, some of the criticisms of the Group's tactics are misplaced. It is wrong, for example, to maintain that the increase in family allowances for poorer families was paid exclusively by richer families. The 1967/68 increase in family allowances resulted in a net £121 million increase in expenditure which was paid for from general taxation. Half of all the families, however, received no additional increase in income as a result of the changes, and their enthusiasm for further increases in family allowances accompanied by claw-back was necessarily limited.

The Group was nonetheless the main stimulus behind demands for the child benefit scheme, believing this to be the most effective way of helping poor families. Yet the child benefit scheme itself lays the basis for a family lobby. (Families are defined here as those households with children, and this definition excludes the idea of an extended family as the basis for a family lobby.) With the abolition of child tax allowances, the child benefit took on a dual function: as a means of combating family poverty and as the instrument by which chancellors could maintain equity in tax-free income between those with children and the childless, irrespective of the level of income of the household.

This section looks at the development of those ideas which have formed the intellectual base of a family lobby in this country, ideas which became politically relevant with the introduction of the child benefit scheme. It then goes on to examine briefly the political birth of Britain's family lobby. The third theme consists of a retrospective view on what has been happening to the relative living standards of families over the period when CPAG was campaigning, for much of the time, for measures benefiting only the poor. The section ends with an outline of what should be a family lobby's next campaigns.

Intellectual base for a family lobby

The disadvantage of families in the fiscal and benefit systems was first highlighted in the late 1960s in the work of Margaret Wynn and Della Nevitt. In their separate ways these two scholars began to make a major contribution to the debate by plotting the relative decline of living standards of households with children. Their work makes a fascinating case study of how the growth of a set of ideas outside the political system eventually becomes the basis for a major political campaign. The bridge over which these ideas were brought into the political system was the child benefit scheme.

Margaret Wynn

Margaret Wynn's work made two main points.(1) The first was to draw attention to the minority of households who are at any one time responsible for children. Updating these figures we find that, in 1980, 13 per cent of dependent children lived in 2 per cent of households, 36 per cent of dependent children in 8 per cent of households and 80 per cent of dependent children in 23 per cent of households. At the present time, only 38 per cent of households have the responsibility for raising the next generation.

Margaret Wynn's second major contribution was to question whether the living standards of families were adequate for their needs. The theme is taken up in Chapter 8, 'The Minimum Needs of Children', an essay that was an important watershed in changing the Group's emphasis (at least in the period up to 1980) from a poverty to a family lobby. It examines the way Rowntree defined poverty in his first and major study of poverty in York and shows that while observers have taken him to have devised an absolute standard of poverty, it was in fact a relative measurement. The essay also questions how accurate the measurement of children's and women's needs are in the Rowntree calculations.

In his first study — just before the turn of the century — Rowntree's poverty line income was presented as a calculation on a minimum level of income that would provide for 'mere physical efficiency'. Food made up the largest part of such a budget, and for his calculations on food needs Rowntree relied on the work of the American nutritionist, Atwater. Atwater's calculations were mainly concerned with the needs of adult males and he arbitrarily guessed the relative needs of women and children, setting both as a proportion of the adult male's food requirements. On this aspect of his calculations Atwater himself observed:

> As a rule a woman requires less food than a man, and the amount required by children is still less, varying with age. It is customary to assign certain factors which shall represent the amount of nutrients required by children of different ages and by women as compared with adult men.

The rates for children ranged from 0.3 for a child under two years old, to 0.8 of the adult equivalent for children aged between 14 and 16 years. Atwater concluded with the following key statement:

> These factors are based in part upon experimental data and in part upon arbitrary assumptions. They are subject to revision when experimental evidence shall warrant more definite conclusions.(2)

Rowntree did not question these relativities even though he observed that they should be revised as more evidence became available. Much the same overall relativities were evident in the major revisions to his poverty calculations carried out in the mid-1930s. And while Beveridge made minor adjustments to the formula, the disadvantage of women and children to men was enshrined in the Beveridge Report's recommendations. From there they passed, unchallenged, into the benefit rates of the post-war welfare state. The assumptions underlying Rowntree's and Beveridge's work also affected the relativities in the tax system, although, fortunately, to a lesser extent.

Della Nevitt

It was the effect of these relativities in the fiscal benefit system which Della Nevitt began to record in her work dating back to the 1960s. Like Margaret Wynn, Della Nevitt has made a major contribution to the understanding of the relative living standards of households of different composition. She began her contribution when researching for the Milner Holland Report into housing conditions in London. In the first instance, she was asked to address herself to the question of how far tenants could afford to pay rent increases. To answer this required a knowledge of net living standards after taking into account the payment of taxes and benefits. Side by side with an analysis of the net disposable income of tenants, Della Nevitt undertook a similar analysis for owner-occupiers. At this early stage she began to identify the distributional impact of tax benefits and local authority subsidies and how these operated against the background of differences in disposable income left by the payment of taxes and the gaining of benefits.

The next stage in the development of these ideas came when

working on a review of local government finance for the then Ministry of Housing and Local Government. Here, Della Nevitt's work showed that no major changes in the distribution of subsidies (and the consequential increase in council house rents) could justly occur without additional support being given to families with children in the council-house sector. This view was based on her analysis of the operation of the existing taxes and benefits system, which had so penalised families with children that there were no additional resources in family budgets to meet further rent increases.

The third stage of her work was undertaken in conjunction with Jonathan Bradshaw of the University of York. A computer simulation model was set up to look at the relative living standards of households of different composition, after taking into account the net effect of any changes in benefits or taxation. Describing the results of the computer run-outs Bradshaw has remarked that the figures spoke for themselves: how much families had lost out could be clearly seen from the tables.

Although Jonathan Bradshaw had been a member of the Group's Executive since 1971, the ideas of Della Nevitt and Margaret Wynn on the relative living standards of families had developed independently of the poverty lobby in general and CPAG in particular. Why was it that so little use was made of their findings, at least up till 1976? Part of the explanation is that it was difficult for a poverty lobby, which had designed the claw-back principle so that any help was limited to low income families, to begin emphasising the issue of horizontal equity until the interests of richer and poorer families could be once again aligned. This occurred with the introduction of child benefits, and this change was reflected in the Group's campaigns.

Political birth of the family lobby

The child benefit scheme has its immediate roots in the Conservative Government's tax credit proposals. In October 1972 the Heath Government published a Green Paper entitled *Proposals for a Tax Credit System*. In the foreword to the Green Paper the Government argued that:

> The tax credit system is a reform which embodies the socially valuable device of paying tax credits, to the extent that they are not used up against tax due, positively as benefit. The system is therefore a practical expression of the desire shown by all political parties to provide better

> support for those who, because of family responsibilities, economic circumstances or advancing years, are hard-pressed.(3)

The Green Paper went on to argue that the individual and the community stood in close relationship with one another through the twin systems of PAYE and social security benefit. The PAYE system was concerned with what people pay in tax, and the social security system is concerned with what support a person receives in benefit. The aim of tax credit proposals, therefore, was

> to build on these two systems and to create a new and simpler system which over a wide part of the field will bring together what people pay and what they receive. It does so in a way which is better for all concerned. Fewer people will be means-tested, and others means-tested less often, and for the community there will be a large saving in administrative staff.(4)

Part of the tax credit proposals concerned the recasting of child tax allowances and family allowances into a new payment — or tax credits — for children. This proposal raised the key question about which of the parents the credits should be paid to. As the Green Paper noted: 'The question whether the child credits should be paid to the father or to the mother, or whether payment should be split between them where there is more than one child, is one of the more important issues raised by the scheme'.(5)

Somewhat ingenuously the Green Paper attempted to set out the merits of the status quo by way of a statement which, while having immediately explosive political consequences, played an important part in starting to bring together many disparate groups into a family lobby.(6) Indeed had one deliberately set about writing a statement in order to give rise to the political repercussions which were to follow, one couldn't have devised a more suitable form of words. The relevant section from the Green Paper reads as follows:

> Although the Government regard the issue as entirely open . . . it has been assumed . . . that the recipient of tax credits would be the father. This is only because, so far as the tax structure is concerned, the child credit would replace child tax allowances and because this is the simplest form of the scheme to describe.(7)

Prompt reaction

The reaction of poverty groups, women's organisations and feminist groups was immediate. Child credits became an issue of some political importance and, against mounting public opposition, the

Government quickly retreated and promised that the credits would be paid to mothers.

This 'concession' had major repercussions on the whole tax credit proposals. In one sense the Green paper was right to think of paying the credits to fathers; the original idea was for the credits to be offset against tax liabilities, and more fathers than mothers are currently in work. But powerful emotions and economic realities are tied up with the payment of children's allowances to mothers, although sadly the political impact of this feeling has so far been felt only in a negative way, against the loss of family allowance payments to the mother, and not in a positive way that might help to forge a family lobby. The Government's peace-offering to mothers effectively partitioned-off the child tax credit and paved the way for the introduction of a separate child credit or, as it later became known, child benefit scheme.

Labour's 1973 programme contained a commitment to introduce a new benefit (which later became known as child benefit) separate from a tax credit scheme, as part of an attack on family poverty. But the child benefit scheme, although designed primarily as a measure to combat family poverty, was also to act as a catalyst of the family movement — in the sense that the sharp elbows of the middle class, defending their own interests, were, contingently, to protect the interests of poorer families. The abolition of tax allowances for children means that horizontal tax equity, i.e. maintaining a fair distribution of the tax burden between the childless taxpayers and those with children whatever the level of income, can only be maintained by way of increases in child benefit. These increases were also important as a means of tackling family poverty, and so the poverty and family lobby are joined in a common interest. Moreover, by emphasising the needs of all families, the child benefit scheme completed a circle began by the Family Endowment Society and Eleanor Rathbone.

Families lost out

The evidence now shows that during the period when the Group was campaigning for help for poor families three powerful forces were at work which put all families at a disadvantage compared to childless households. (It could be argued that the recent deterioration in the family's position is at least partly due to the exclusivity of the Group's poverty campaigns.) These forces, which are identified in 'Penalising All Children' (Chapter 9) require only a summary and updating here.

First, there have been significant changes in the burden of taxation. Elsewhere I have tried to identify how the tax burden has moved against low income groups as well as shifting an increased burden onto taxpayers with children, irrespective of whether these taxpayers are rich or poor.(8) Low income households with children have therefore suffered a double disadvantage.

Changes in the tax threshold

One way of looking at the increasing tax burden is to examine changes in the tax threshold. Over the post-war period the tax threshold as measured against average earnings has fallen for all groups of taxpayers, but has fallen fastest for those taxpayers with children. The reason for this, over most of the post-war period, was that the value of child tax allowances was allowed to decline faster than the real value of other tax allowances. For example, the value of CTAs in 1957/58 — the year when age-related allowances were introduced — as a proportion of the single person's allowances, stood at 71.4 per cent for children not over 11, 89.3 per cent for children over 11 but not over 16, and 101.7 per cent for children over 16. By 1976/77 they had fallen to 40.8 per cent, 45.2 per cent and 49.6 per cent respectively of the single person's allowance, and these figures take no account of claw-back. As 'Penalising All Children' goes on to show, this decline has not been uniform over the whole period.

One consequence of increasing the relative tax burden of families with children has been to tax such households even though their income is below the official poverty line. Two poverty lines are relevant to this analysis: the supplementary benefit poverty line and the eligibility level for FIS. As we can see from Table 6.1 the tax threshold is below both the supplementary benefit level for all types of taxpayers and also below the FIS level. This results in the absurd

Table 6.1 Tax threshold and poverty line incomes, 1981

(1) No. of children	*(2)* SB level	FIS level	*(3)* tax threshold
1	67.15	£74	£41.25
2	75.05	£82	£41.25
3	82.95	£90	£41.25

(1) under 11
(2) assuming an average rent payment of £11.90.
(3) wife not working and tax threshold relates to the April of each year and the benefit thresholds to the November.

situation where some poor working families are paid FIS by the DHSS because of their low income, and yet this FIS payment is partially and sometimes even totally wiped out by income tax charges levied by the Inland Revenue.

Inflation

The second force at work affecting the relative living standards of families has been the differential impact of inflation. Officially inflation is measured by the movement of the Department of Employment's retail price index (RPI). Each month the Department reports on the rate of change of price increases and this is usually interpreted as the measurement of inflation. However, the RPI records only the average rate of change in the level of prices over a vast range of goods and services. Moreover, the basket of goods and services used by the Department of Employment is said to reflect an average household, yet John Muellbauer has estimated that the RPI weights correspond to households about 70 per cent of the way up the income distribution.(9)

In evidence to the Royal Commission on the Distribution of Income and Wealth the Low Pay Unit detailed how the cost of necessities has tended to increase faster than the overall price level. Since low-income groups as well as families devote a larger proportion of their budget to these items, the cost of living for the poorest households, and families, has risen more rapidly than that of households in general, while the cost of living of higher income groups, and those without children, has increased more slowly.

'Penalising All Children' details the evidence from the Low Pay Unit and also the work of David Piachaud, who examined the differential impact of inflation for large families on a low income for the period 1956 to the middle of 1975. More recent work from Chris Pond still shows the differential impact of inflation working against those on low incomes. In the six months up to August 1980, retail prices for the low paid increased by 7.7 per cent while those for the high paid rose by 6.4 per cent.

In a fair society an increase in the burden of taxation, and a differential effect of price increases (both forces working against the interests of families) would have been compensated by extra increases in benefit levels. In fact, the reverse has occurred. Whereas pensions, for example, have been increased on twenty two occasions since the Second World War, family allowances/child benefits have been increased on only nine occasions. In addition, most increases in

Table 6.2 Indices of real income after taxes and transfers by household type 1962, 1976–1978 (1962 = 100)

	1 adult pensioner (b)	*2 adult pensioner (b)*	*1 adult non-pensioner (c)*	*2 adult non-pensioner (c)*	*2 adults, 2 children*	*2 adults, 4 children*
1962	100	100	100	100	100	100
1976	184	180	144	134	128	133
1977	181	177	144	132	127	123
1978	192	185	151	145	142	139

Sources: DHSS *Abstract of Statistics for Index of Retail Prices, Average Earnings, Social Security Benefits and Contributions*, May 1980 (for prices).
Economic Trends, January 1977 pp107–110.

Notes: (a) Disposable income less indirect taxes plus food and housing subsidies deflated by the Retail Price Index (Disposable income = original income plus cash benefits less direct taxes).
(b) Pensioner households are defined as those where more than three-quarters of household income consists of National Insurance pensions and supplementary allowances to such pensions.
(c) Includes some retired households — see note (b).

family allowances/child benefit have been small both in percentage and in real terms compared with the increases in pensions. As the evidence in 'The Minimum Needs of Children' (see Chapter 8) shows, the level of child support — which has never kept pace with the increases in other benefits — was itself introduced below the level proposed by the wartime Coalition Government, which was itself at a lower level than that advocated in the Beveridge Report.

The effect of these forces in reducing the relative living standards of households with children is shown in a table originally reproduced in 'Penalising All Children' and brought up to date in Table 6.2. The analysis takes 1962 as a base year. While the increase in expenditure on child benefits from 1976 onwards is beginning to have an effect on the relative incomes of families with children, this group is still at a major disadvantage compared with childless households. By 1977 the real income of an adult, after taking into account taxes and the payment of benefit, had risen from 100 in 1962 to 144 in 1977. For two-adult households with two and four children their real income had risen to only 127 and 123 respectively. A year later, by 1978, the real income level of a single person had risen to 151 compared to 142 and 139 of households with two and four children respectively. This improvement occurred at a time when decision makers and opinion leaders were becoming more aware about the needs of all families and not just poor families.

What next?

One of the themes of this essay has been the difficulty of raising new interests in a political system dominated by class issues. Yet I believe the tide is beginning to run in favour of the development of a powerful family lobby. Paradoxically, one reason for this belief stems from the economic difficulties we find ourselves in today. On the face of it this could indicate that there was little scope for new initiatives, particularly for one which occupies an obvious class base. But in this sense, the end of economic growth could help to bring about a major revolution in British politics.

Since the war there has been a fundamental consensus between the major parties on their approach to redistribution. The formula was set out most clearly by Anthony Crosland who believed that a steadily rising national income allowed the rich to remain rich while financing programmes to help the poor. As 'Poverty, Growth and the Redistribution of Income' (Chapter 11) shows, powerful forces are at work — both economic and demographic — which now rule out this option. To follow the Croslandite view, of putting a radical programme of reform on ice while awaiting the return of growth, will result in cuts in living standards of the poor.

The redistribution debate

The political debate therefore turns on how to redistribute existing resources. Elsewhere I have outlined the need for a four-fold redistribution, from rich to poor, from men to women, from the state to the individual, and the spreading of resources from the most affluent periods of the life cycle to those of relative deprivation.(10)

It is this last form of redistribution which could foster the growth of interest in a family lobby. One of the big political questions facing us over the next twenty years will be how can one's lifetime's earnings, which are gained in a period of up to forty years, be spread over a lifetime which now often exceeds eighty years. Clearly, a system of income support needs to be developed for those periods when households have children and when the breadwinners are retired. This forges a natural link between families and pensioners and should prevent one being played off against the other.

Falling living standards

A second stimulus for a family lobby may also arise from the present economic difficulties. The historian of the pre-war campaign for family allowances, John Macnicol, explains the demise of the campaign for families in the post-war world in the following terms.

> Various reasons have been put forward, such as the disappearance of the demographic argument thanks to the rise in the birth-rate (from 13.9 per thousand population in 1941 to 18.0 in 1962), but the most important factors were probably low unemployment and rising real wages.(11)

As unemployment continues to mount, and as it is unlikely that real wages will be maintained in the immediate future, the necessity of a renewed campaign to protect the living standards of families with children becomes more urgent. Hopefully this will be fed by a growing public realisation of the extent to which households responsible for children have received lower increases in real incomes than other groups when times were more prosperous.

Incentive – a double-edged argument

A third factor could help the emergence of a family lobby.

According to Macnicol, the need to maintain and improve the incentives to work was one of the main reasons accounting for the Government's (and particularly the Treasury's) U-turn on the family allowance scheme. Macnicol again picks up the story here:

> the Second World War undoubtedly speeded up trends that were in evidence in the late 1930s, when there was a growing consensus among social policy experts that (a) the social services needed a drastic reorganisation, and (b), in such reorganisation the problem of men with large families being better off financially when unemployed than when employed needed to be tackled by the introduction of family allowances.(12)

Both forces could be mobilised in support of the development of a family lobby today. There is growing dissatisfaction with the way the traditional benefit welfare state works, and in part this dissatisfaction is linked to the 'incentives to work' question. This argument is one which the poverty lobby has thought is wise not to press too strongly. Although the 'poverty trap' debate is essentially about incentives, and although this argument has been used fairly extensively, its use has been in aid of wage rises and/or child benefit increases, and has been centred almost totally on the low paid in work.

There is however another side of the incentives argument which is little used by radical reformers, and this relates to the incentive to take work if it is available. Largely in an attempt to prevent the argument from being forged into a weapon and being used against the poor, the poverty lobby has understandably stressed how few people are better-off out of work than in work. Emphasising the point, the Supplementary Benefits Commission estimated at the end of 1975 that 'only slightly more than 1 per cent of all families where the head was either self-employed or in full-time work would have been entitled to a higher income on supplementary benefit than in work'.(13)

What has been left out of the argument is the extent to which large numbers of people are *little* better off and are sometimes worse off in work. How this happens can be seen from the following example.(14) In early 1981 a married couple with two children aged 4 and 6 gained a basic unemployment benefit including earnings related supplement of £44.49 a week. Additions for child benefit, the national insurance additions for children, rent and rate rebates, free school meals and a tax refund brought this income to a level of £83.20. From this would be deducted rent and rates giving a total net income for the family when unemployed of £70.85.

The same family, if the head of the household was offered work at a gross level of £95 a week would, after taking into account child benefit, rent and rate rebates, but minus tax, national insurance contributions, the payment of rents, rates and quite modest expenses to work (£3.55), have a net weekly spending power of £67.95 a week. Again, the reason why families are caught in low incomes is the way means-tested help is clawed back from them as their income rises over a whole range of income levels. The income range over which families find themselves little better off by taking a job is now very considerable. Similarly, once in work, the 'poverty trap' operates in such a way that it is very difficult for working families to improve their *net* income to any significant extent.

For the reasons already described, poverty groups have been, quite understandably, loath to push this incentives argument. But, to use Jonathan Bradshaw's phrase, this poverty plateau now is so extensive that a much more radical campaign is called for. To deal effectively with the incentives issue can mean truly massive wage increases, yet such a move will benefit those without children in the same measure as those with, even though the incentives issue is almost exclusively limited to households with children. Alternatively, a minimum wage approach can be linked to a generous system of child benefits. This campaign, in turn, can be linked into the need to spread the earnings of forty years to meet more adequately one's family responsibilities which fall over a minority of these years. There are risks in developing a campaign along these lines (for some politicians might increase their campaign for cuts in unemployment benefit), but the campaign in the 1970s, resulting in a massive increase in child benefit, also involved risks which many radicals believed should not have been taken.

Shifting the tax burden

Redistributing resources over a lifetime will not preclude other forms of redistribition. It will still be important to consider ways of traditional vertical redistribution from richer to poorer groups in society. One argument used against such redistribution is that the resources over which the rich have command are small in comparison to the needs of the rest of society, and that a vertical redistribution would have very little effect on the living standards of those lower down the income scale. There would still be a moral case for redistribtion even if this charge were true. But as the essay

'Limits to Redistribution' (Chapter 12) tries to show, the tax burden has been shifting in two directions during the last twenty years or so. It has been moved down vertically onto those on lower and lower income while also being pushed horizontally onto taxpayers with children. Despite this two-fold shift in the incidence of taxation, the major tax-cutting budgets of the Thatcher Government redistributed resources to those on higher incomes and made no distinction between taxpayers with children and the childless. The 1979 budget, for example, reduced taxation by £4.6 billion, of which the richest 7 per cent picked up 34 per cent of the tax handouts. Some families benefited by the increase in the married man's allowance but there was no way by which the Chancellor made any additional tax cuts to families with children. To have done so would have resulted in an increasing child benefit which the Chancellor ruled out on public expenditure grounds.

There will be powerful forces at work to reverse these tax cuts in the early days of the next Labour Government. The case is now being made within the labour movement that it is not only poorer taxpayers who should benefit from any shift in the tax burden back onto those with higher incomes, but that also families with children should be key beneficiaries.

Family-interest organisations

There are also organisational changes which will favour the development of a family lobby. Already two organisations exist which are trying to promote the interests of families, and particularly their financial well-being. One of these, the Study Commission on the Family, acts as a standing unofficial Royal Commission gathering, publishing data on what is happening to the family in Britain today and, equally important, what has been happening over the past couple of decades. The Commission's publications are beginning to play an important educative role among politicians and the media, and could play an even more important part if the resources were found to enable the findings to reach a wider public. The second organisation, the Family Forum, is an umbrella group for those voluntary bodies taking an interest in families with children. The Forum is taking on a permanent institutional form, and could play a key part in helping to give shape to a family lobby. Either or both of these organisations should now try and widen their base and involve families at a grass-roots level, and so help to crystallise and channel politically the legitimate demands of households with children.

Both organisations also need to get a commitment from the political parties on two issues which will build a family consciousness into the political process. The issuing by government of a family impact statement to accompany each major change in official policy will begin to make politicians, civil servants and the media more aware of the needs of households with children.(15) Likewise, the commissioning of budgetary surveys, similar to those in Europe and the USA, will again help to change the tempo of public debate on the unmet needs of families.

Conclusion

The tale of the slowly emerging family lobby is the most important event described in these pages. It holds out the hope, not only of bringing about a greater fairness in the tax and benefit system but, in so doing, abolishing family poverty as we know it today. To achieve both of these goals there will be a need for a major vertical and horizontal redistribution of income.

The obstacles to achieving either of these objectives should not be underestimated. One issue which must be tackled first is the myth that there has been a major redistribution from rich to poor in the post-war world. The 'Limits to Redistribution' paper (Chapter 12) tries to set out the extent and nature of the vertical redistribution of income over the past thirty years or so. Here is a theme to which left politics will have to return time and time again over the next few years.

Likewise, the Left will have to accept that the post-war political consensus would have come to an end without the vigorous help of Mrs Thatcher. Thanks largely to the unprecedented growth in national income after the Second World War, the Labour Party's programme could be financed from part of the product of this growth. But the world-wide depression in the 1970s and 1980s has put paid to this approach in a way which is still not fully realised. 'Poverty, Growth and the Redistribution of Income' (Chapter 11) looks at how the current depression with consequential increases in unemployment together with demographic changes giving rise to a 6 per cent annual increase in one parent families, calls for a redistribution of *existing* resources if the living standards of the poor are not to fall in real terms.

The campaign for a vertical redistribution of income from richer to poorer households ought to be joined to demands for greater horizontal equity in the distribution of current resources. How the earnings of a working life are to spread over an entire lifetime must be made into one of the key political issues of the 1980s. In launching this debate the role of the family lobby will be crucial.

The full implementation of the child benefit scheme — with all its revolutionary consequences on the distribution of income not only between rich and poor but, of equal importance, between men and women, adults and children and over each person's lifetime — is now tied up with establishing an effective family lobby. Should such a lobby fail to take root then the cause of poor parents might well be lost. If the sharp elbows of the middle classes are not forged into an effective family lobby the biggest losers will be poor families.

PART II

Campaigning Essays

7 Three Political Pieces

The following articles were important in helping to change the political debate on poverty. The first, 'An Incomes Policy for Families', was the draft which formed the basis for CPAG's campaign 'The Poor Get Poorer Under Labour' in 1970. Its political stance began a new phase in CPAG's campaigning activities. 'The Poverty Trap' article, written with David Piachaud, also had important political ramifications which are described in the first half of the book. The poverty trap debate made relevant to trade union leaders, as never before, CPAG's programme on universal support for families. 'Killing a Commitment' had a major political impact of a different kind. The publication of this article based on Cabinet minutes caused a political storm the repercussions of which are still being felt today. This leak of Cabinet papers made child benefit a major political issue and ensured, as far as any action could, the introduction of the scheme. The publication also put politicians of both parties on the defensive in respect to income support schemes for families. Senior politicians may not have been genuinely converted in support of the scheme, but they are careful when dealing with child benefits, for fear of another political explosion equal to that following what *The Observer* called the most extensive leak of Cabinet papers this century.

An Incomes Policy for Families

Beliefs and performance of a Labour Government

Labour's tradition

At the end of 1964, the British electorate voted into power the third Labour administration since the Second World War. Its advent was accompanied by a considerable amount of public 'goodwill' and there was the expectation — built up over the previous thirteen years, as well as from the traditional beliefs of the Labour movement — that it was going to act very differently from its predecessor, especially in protecting and advancing the interests of the least privileged. To a sizeable part of the electorate, the Party clearly stood for the underdog, and according to its own publications it rejected the Tory Party's acceptance of poverty in the midst of plenty, a society which 'allowed the weakest to go to the wall'.

Not that the Party underestimated the size of poverty in Britain. A document published in 1961 estimated that between 7 and 8 million were living close to the poverty line. But the Party's determination to tackle this problem was summed up by the Prime Minister, who spoke, in the election year, of the 'burning desire', among Labour Party members at all levels, to abolish poverty. After five years, the Labour Government's actions have not matched up to expectations.

The Government claims that this is due to events outside their control. True, they inherited a severe economic crisis, but it was always on the cards that this would happen. For example, John Strachey forecast that 'unless we are quite fantastically lucky . . . the next Labour Government will come into office in a situation in which, if it even attempts to implement social reforms, 'fair shares' programmes, without doing anything else, the national reserves of gold, dollars and foreign exchange will pour out of the country in a torrent'.

In the event, the economic crisis was already awaiting the 1964 Labour administration, but this is no excuse for postponing so much of the anti-poverty programme. In 1945 the Attlee administration was confronted with an even graver economic situation but it proved able to implement the whole of its reforming programme before the 1950 election. That Government 'took over a country in an appalling condition. Industry, transport and commerce had been distorted to serve the war effort. Overseas investment had been practically all spent, the merchant navy was tragically reduced, millions of homes and other properties had been destroyed, 6 million men and women were scattered across the world in the services'. Yet 'all these obstacles were tackled and overcome by the most energetic administration the country has ever known'. And 'while this remarkable recovery was being effected, Labour at the same time put its socialism into practice. The Health Service and National Insurance was established, Family Allowances were first paid, new industry was located where it was most needed, new towns were started and legal aid services were introduced — and there were many other long-awaited reforms'. With such a record there was little need for Government supporters to scale down their expectations of what would eventually be achieved by this Government. Indeed, a recurring theme in its handouts was that the Party 'stands . . . for a society in which the claims of those in hardship or distress come first'.

Strategy against poverty

Just as the Labour Party accepted the size of the poverty problem, so it conceded that a whole strategy had to be designed if it was ever going to be successfully tackled. This strategy was to go well beyond the spheres of traditional social security measures. There was a need for a restructuring of the educational system along comprehensive lines, the urgent necessity to provide decent homes and link this to a regional economic policy and the need to review the structure and share of resources to the health service. Of course, all these demands had to compete with each other for scarce resources, but allocations would be made rationally and within the compass of a national plan.

Even within the social security field, several different but related policies were planned in order to combat existing inequalities. There was to be a guaranteed minimum income, laying down a new national minimum benefit so that all those whose income fell below the new minimum would receive *as of right* an income supplement. The near certainty of poverty in old age for the majority of the population was to be abolished by the introduction of a wage-related pension. The same principle was to extend to sickness and unemployment, and the 'sting' was to be taken out of redundancy by the establishment of a National Severance Pay Scheme.

Interim measures

Once in office, the Government showed considerable courage. In his first Budget on 11 November 1964, Mr Callaghan announced details of proposed increases in National Insurance and associated benefits. Since then the Government has raised National Insurance and Supplementary Benefits levels a number of times, and in real terms they stand at 20 per cent above their value in 1964. However, the nation was told that the November increases were an interim measure while the Government undertook a major review of the whole social security system. This announcement was a disappointment to many; as late as October 1963, the Labour Party Conference had been told that the Party's programme had been based on 'detailed and rigorous technical, financial and actuarial advice'. Indeed the idea of a major review first appeared in the Conservative Party's 1964 election manifesto and they had been in office continuously for thirteen years.

As with the improvement in the position of the '10*s*' widow, the Government has implemented a number of promised reforms. A short-term wage-related unemployment and sickness pay scheme is in operation and Parliament is now considering the long-term restructuring of other National Insurance benefits. At another time we will wish to comment in detail on how the former measures are working, but this should not detract from the credit due to the Government for introducing many needed reforms in the face of bitter opposition in the press and in some sections of Parliament.

Family poverty package deal

The Child Poverty Action Group's main interest has been the Government's proposals to combat family poverty and other measures which vitally affect the poor. The report, *Circumstances of Families* (1966), showed that half a million families, having one and a quarter million children, lived on or below the official poverty line. It also clearly illustrated the size of the 'notch' problem, i.e. those living just beyond the official poverty line. An increase of 60s above Supplementary Benefits scales accounted for one sixth of all family budgets.

After nearly two years of reviewing the different alternatives, the Government announced the results of their deliberations. Family allowances were to be increased by 7s but this was to be part of a package deal. At the same time, the price of school meals and welfare milk was to be raised, but families with four or more dependent children were entitled to at least one free school dinner. According to the Government's own calculations these measures would bring only half of the poorest families up to basic Supplementary Benefit level.

Making the poor pay

Regressive taxation

The position of the poor can also be vitally affected by the way revenue is raised to finance improved social services. Both the present Prime Minister (Harold Wilson) and Secretary of State for Social Services (Richard Crossman) have in the past condemned the raising of National Insurance contributions. Mr Crossman in the early months of 1963 spoke of 'a flat rate increase of 1s for low-paid workers [as] a heavy imposition indeed. So heavy is the burden put on the worker by our saying that all workers must pay the same that everybody earning under £15–16 a week is being milked of far more than the share due to him for the rest of the social services . . . Each time the Government puts a shilling on tax they make the burden more intolerable'.

Later in the same year, Mr Crossman went on record as saying, 'You can't possibly allow them [the National Insurance contributions], a flat-rate poll tax on the lower-paid workers, to be increased once again'. These same thoughts were expressed by the Prime Minister in 1965 when he said, 'The Conservatives in the last four years in times of crisis increased stamp contributions to bear most heavily on those whose needs are greatest and whose incomes are lowest'. Over the past five years the Government has increased the National Insurance and Health stamp by over 50 per cent.

Consequences of devaluation

During his devaluation speech on television, the Prime Minister said 'It is the duty of your Government to ensure by special measures that when the burdens have to be borne, those who are liable to be hardest hit are protected, and your Government will fulfil that duty'. So far the only measures designed to protect low income families from the economic effects of devaluation have been an increase of 3*s* per child in family allowances. For an unskilled labourer with three children, this represents an increase of about 2½ per cent in his income. But prices have already risen by more than 10 per cent.

Apart from the consequential rise in prices, other Government measures, introduced because of devaluation (in 1967), have adversely affected the poor. Labour has achieved the longest period of high unemployment for thirty years. National Insurance and National Health Service contributions have been increased. Free school milk in secondary schools has been abolished. Free school dinners for the fourth and subsequent child have been withdrawn, even though this formed one of the two favourable parts of the package deal aimed at abolishing family poverty. Charges for dental and optical services and welfare milk have been increased by 50 per cent and prescription charges, which were abolished in 1965, were re-introduced.

All these measures have been a major defeat for the poor as well as for the Government. The 1964 election manifesto stated emphatically that 'The most serious attack on the Health Service made by Conservative Ministers has been the increased burden of prescription charges imposed by them on those least able to pay'. As well as pledging the party to abolish them, the manifesto concluded the subject by saying 'our aim is to restore as rapidly as possible a completely free Health Service'.

Strictly speaking, the measures resulting from devaluation have not increased the numbers of families whose income falls below the official poverty line, but they have imposed considerable burdens on those least able to stand them. And although it is impossible to calculate the net effect of all these factors on the numbers on or below the statutory poverty line, if any reduction has been achieved, it is certainly less than the 50 per cent predicted in 1967.

So far the main import of this memorandum has been that of all the groups to benefit from this Government's measures, low income families have benefited least — if at all. Whether one takes the 25 per cent increase in prices since 1964 (up till 1970), or the success of the prices and incomes policy in holding down more effectively the wage increases of the lower-paid, the enormous increase in National Insurance contributions, the record level of unemployment, or the numerous measures mentioned in this memorandum, the conclusion is the same. The group that has benefited least from the Labour Government has been the low-income families which are generally believed to be its bedrock supporters. The rest of the memorandum reviews suggested remedies.

Concentrating help on the poor

Means tests

CPAG is totally opposed to an extension of means-tested benefits. Whether one takes rate rebates, prescription charge exemptions, the right to free welfare foods or practically any of the existing poor people's benefits, the story is the same: many poor people do not claim what is theirs by right. To some extent this could be due to the lack of knowledge. There are after all over 1,500 unique local authority means tests. Clear publicity does make a considerable difference to the take-up rate, as the campaign for free school meals demonstrated; but even then there remains a residual number of poor people who refuse to parade their poverty to obtain a State handout. In a very real sense it is a vote of no confidence by the poor in the way they are being offered help. There is a need therefore to look for an alternative course of action.

Negative income tax

In the 1964 election manifesto the Government set out their intention to introduce a guaranteed income for pensioners and widows. For a time CPAG was interested in a similar scheme which sought to extend the benefit of child tax allowances to all families. This modest proposal to concentrate help on those in greatest need was soon swamped by a more elaborate scheme for negative income tax. As the Secretary of State for Social Services spelt out in his Herbert Morrison lecture, the shortcomings of such proposals are now much more apparent. Mr Crossman listed three major objections, with which we are in total agreement.

First, the present tax machinery does not cover a large number of people, and so there are obvious difficulties in using the existing arrangements for adjusting everybody's income up to the required level. Second, the Inland Revenue does not have information on the ownership of capital or on what people pay in rent — an essential piece of data if one wants to guarantee people a certain income to cover their needs. Third, whatever information the taxman has it does not refer to this year's, let alone this week's income. With the circumstances of many poor people changing even weekly, this is obviously the most serious obstacle to implementing a negative income tax.

Of course these objections may one day be overcome, but then we would want to know a lot more about how the proposed system was going to work before we fully endorsed it. In the meantime, one must conclude that, however forceful the discussion, a negative income tax could not possibly be introduced within the next ten years. What can be done then to improve the position of low income families, particularly in the last sixteen months' life of this Government?

A minimum wage

Low wages are the most important cause of family poverty. The recently published data from the Government Earnings Survey showed that just under a million men were earning less than £15 per week. This situation is intolerable and morally the case for a minimum wage is unanswerable. However, the economic effects of such a policy are, to say the least, uncertain. There is the possibility that skilled and managerial unions might force wage increases to maintain existing differentials. Employers might be successful in passing most, if not all, of their increased costs onto the consumer by increased prices. And then there is the danger of adding to the large and growing numbers of the long-term unemployed. Accordingly, imagination needs to be applied to the introduction of a minimum wage. For example, could it be linked to the reform of National Insurance contributions, so that the economic disincentive to employ low-paid workers at the minimum wage is offset by a proportionately lower employer contribution to the National Insurance fund?

In their enthusiasm for a minimum wage, some people argue that the payment should be high enough to keep an average-size family at a reasonable standard of living. We do not concur with these sentiments. A minimum wage should be set at the same level as Supplementary Benefit rates for a married couple with one child and, say, a payment of £5 to cover the weekly rent. In order to ensure that the minimum wage keeps pace with the rising cost of living we would also propose that it be linked with the Supplementary Benefit Review machinery. Family allowances for the second and subsequent children should then be made high enough to cover the cost of all children but the first. Taking a weighted average of the Supplementary Benefit payment for children, family allowances would need to be in the region of 35s per week.

Linking a minimum wage to Supplementary Benefit level would mean a wage rate of 7s 6d per hour or about £15 per week. In every sense this would be a minimum wage. Evidence from our local branches of individual Supplementary Benefit claimants, or from official Government statistics, shows the inability of even the most able families to budget successfully on Supplementary Benefit income for any length of time. Indeed, the Supplementary Benefit Commission gives *de facto* recognition to this fact by granting discretionary lump sum payments to meet *ad hoc* family requirements. Even so, this modest reform would cost £3,800,000,000 in the first year of operation.

Family allowances

As the possible problems of introducing a minimum wage become more apparent, Barbara Castle's suggestion of a minimum wage by stages looks the most likely way of advance. But by staggering its introduction over a number of years, the need for an extra supplement to incomes becomes even more important. We would therefore advocate extending family allowances to the first child. Not that we wish this to be thought of as an interim measure. With payment for each child, the system of family support would appear more equitable on a number of counts. First, financial support to richer families in tax allowances starts with the first child. Second, for the ordinary family, the arrival of children often causes their first financial crisis. To withhold payment at this point is not only unreasonable but positively harmful. Furthermore, any foreseeable minimum wage would be set at around Supplementary Benefit level, and so there will be an urgent need to increase the incentive to work. Family allowance for the first child would achieve this.

The cost of increasing family allowances to 35s per child including the first would be £115 million per year if the claw-back procedure was extended. In 1968, the Government accepted this proposal of CPAG and adjusted child tax allowances so that the standard-rate tax payer lost the whole of the family allowance increase. Only those families with incomes around or below the average derived any net benefit from the changes, and the maximum benefit went only to a relatively small number of families with extremely low incomes. This effect was described by the Chancellor of the Exchequer as 'a civilised and acceptable form of selectivity'. It is also undeniably an efficient form, since all those intended to benefit did so, in contrast to the conventional type of selective (i.e. means-tested) benefit which invariably fails to reach a high proportion of those entitled.

To the economic advantages of the claw-back principle can be added those of equity. Because of child tax allowances, the Government lost in 1967/68 four times as much as it paid out in family allowances. Thanks to partial implementation of CPAG's claw-back proposals, the ratio is now two to one. This is still inequitable; the extension of claw-back to the whole of the tax allowance would not only fulfil the promise the Chancellor made in 1968 but would create equal pay for all children.

Useful as the 'give and take' method is as a way of giving urgently needed help to the poorest families, its long-term implications are perhaps even more important. It represents a move away from the limited conception of the community's responsibility in relation to family incomes, as merely incidental to either the relief of poverty or the equitable distribution of the tax burden; and towards a clearer recognition of the interest of the community in the welfare of all children, rich and poor. In the context of such a policy of support for families bringing up children, and not just for poor families or income-tax payers, it is clearly right that the community should concern itself with the broader social aspects of childbearing, and in particular with the provision of family planning facilities in the interests of both the individual family and the community.

The incentive to work

It is disturbing that the obsessive desire of Mr Crossman's Department to provide incentives to work have manifested themselves not in substantial increases in family allowances but in an increased establishment of special investigators. This last move, like earlier measures to drive men back to work, is a shameful admission that the Government has failed to keep family allowances at an adequate level. Although Mr Crossman has argued that increases in Supplementary Benefit must be accompanied by increases in family allowances, if an incentive to work is to be retained, the Government has increased family allowances by only 10s per child while Supplementary Benefits have been raised by 19s for a dependent 17-year old.

The failure to pay family allowances for the first child accentuates this difference. In arguing that a minimum wage should provide for a man, wife and one child, while calling for the extension of family allowances for the first child, we wish to ensure that there is every incentive to work. If the Government is so keen to combat workshyness, it should use the simple device of family allowances, which are paid to a man when he is working but are deducted from his supplementary allowance when he is not, as its main weapon.

Summary

We propose that family allowances should be raised to 35s per child per week and that the benefit should extend to the first child.

We argued the need for this reform in the following terms:

1. We accept that the Labour Government inherited an economic crisis in 1964 and that in spite of this it has introduced many urgent reforms. However, we have tried to show that one of the major problems still facing the Government is the existence of family poverty. Indeed many of the Government's own actions have exacerbated it. Low income families have been the group which has benefited least from a Labour Government and the most effective way of getting help to this group is by increasing family allowances.

2. Various alternative solutions were reviewed. An extension of means-tested benefits was dismissed, not only because this policy would be ineffective. It would also be socially divisive and this is just as important an objection. As there seems no possibility of introducing a negative income tax in the foreseeable future, we went on to explore the relationship between the minimum wage policy and a substantial increase in family allowances.

3. Family allowances by themselves could not be successful in eradicating family poverty. Each head of household needs to earn a minimum wage of around Supplementary Benefit level for husband, wife and one child plus a rent payment, otherwise family allowances would need to be set at a prohibitive level.

4. The need to extend family allowances for the first child was not only seen in the terms of increasing the incentive to work. All family allowance payments do this. Extension to the first child would not only make the system seem more equitable to the layman but would protect working class families at one of the critical financial periods in their life cycle.

5. To increase family allowances to 35s including the first child would do more than any other action to redeem the Government's promise to protect the poorest families from the economic effects of devaluation, as well as providing the help for poor families which the Labour movement has traditionally expected from its Government.

The Poverty Trap

Frank Field and David Piachaud

Hundreds of thousands of trade unionists are not getting what they bargained for. It is now a fact that for millions of low-paid workers very substantial pay increases have the absurd effect of increasing only marginally their family's net income and in some cases actually make the family worse off. We have reached the position where it is positively detrimental to many members' interests for the general unions to negotiate large wage increases. What should trade unions be asking for in this situation?

The cause of the present state of affairs lies in the government's polarising pursuit of selectivity and a means-test society. The narrowness of its view of poverty has created a poverty trap. As a family's income increases not only does more tax have to be paid but entitlement to those benefits, available only to the poorest, is lost, On every additional pound received in pay there may be an extra 35 pence in income tax and national insurance to be paid. For every additional pound earned the government's new family income supplement is reduced by 50 pence. These considerations alone may leave a family only 15 pence better off after a £1 pay increase.

And this is not all. As earnings increase, school meals cease to be free and 60 pence per week has to be paid for them for each child. Exemptions too are lost; prescription charges, for example, have to be met in full. Taking everything into account, a low-income family may well be worse off if earnings rise. For such a family, higher wages profit nothing.

In 1970 the TUC argued for a minimum wage of £16.50 per week for all workers; this year they are seeking a minimum of £20 per week. In Table 7.1 the net incomes of single people and of one-, two- and three-child families are shown. It will be seen that when the earnings of a single person increase by £3.50 from £16.50 to £20 per week his net income will increase by £2.50 (from £12.20 to £14.70). For

Table 7.1 Net incomes of single people and of families with up to three children* (1971)

	Supplementary Benefit Level	*Earnings £16.50 p.w.*	*Earnings £20 p.w.*	*Earnings £18 p.w. and increased child support*
Single Person	£8.80	£12.20	£14.70	£13.20
One-Child Family	£14.45	£15.20	£16.10	£16.20
Two-Child Family	£16.45	£16.95	£18.15	£18.20
Three-Child Family	£18.45	£18.45	£19.70	£20.20

* Taking into account family allowance, family income supplement, income tax, national insurance, school meal charges and typical housing costs and work expenses.

one-child families, however, the effect is very different. Owing to the loss of family income supplement, income tax and the cost of school meals, an increase in earnings of £3.50 make a one-child family a mere 90 pence better off. Two- and three-child families only gain slightly more from such a large pay increase.

With the present morass of means-tests, single people and childless couples would gain most from the proposed minimum wage. Those in greatest need, families with children, would gain least. There was a time when any pay increase benefited families with children more than single people; that was in the days when there were reduced rates of tax and most men and families paid no tax at all, still less were ensnared by means tests. Now single people and childless couples gain most from pay increases and this enhances the relative deprivation of low-income families.

If prices are taken into account, an increase in earnings of £3.50 — or over 20 per cent — would not have increased the net income of families with children by enough to keep pace with the rise in the cost of living over the last year. If other means-tested benefits were taken into account, the gains from increased earnings would be still less. Further, it may be seen from the table that even with earnings of £20 the net income of the larger families would remain very close to the supplementary benefit level — effectively in poverty.

How can the trade unions spring their low paid members from the government's poverty trap?

There are two possibilities. The first is to try to blast the low-paid out of the means-test net. To achieve this the unions must win increases of up to 40–50 per cent for the low-paid — not a very hopeful prospect at present. Alternatively the trade unions can insist that improvements in benefits should be a normal and important part of the annual wage negotiations. Then, if the Government concedes adequate increases in national insurance benefits and family allowances, wage settlements may be correspondingly reduced. This latter strategy is in the interests of low-paid families, unions, employers and the government.

In effect, increased family allowances should have just as high a priority for trade unions as increased pay. What the unions must appreciate is the fact that benefits for children must be provided not only to the very poorest but to all families (except possibly the very richest); and that these benefits must be adequate to ensure that all families at work are substantially above the poverty level. In the last column of the table the net income is shown if (a) earnings were £18 per week, (b) family allowances were extended to the first child and increased to £2 per week per child, (c) child tax allowances were abolished and family allowances freed of tax, and (d) school meals were provided free. All the families with children would actually be better off than if they had earned £20 per week without any increase in family allowances; single people would clearly gain less than they would from a greater pay rise.

In one way, such a strategy is selective. It is deliberately designed to ensure that the families who need it most get more help in keeping pace with the cost of living than they otherwise would. All low-paid households would gain from the strategy by roughly the same amount. The lessons should be clear, even to the government. Family income can be increased more at far less cost if more modest wage rises are linked to substantial increases in family allowances. The poverty trap is, therefore, not only a challenge to the trade union movement. The Government is in the trap as well.

For Sir Keith Joseph to admit the failure of his means-test policy and his family income supplement would mean the abandonment of the core of the Government's social policy. But any success he achieves is bound to lead to a massive trade union offensive to protect their low-paid members which would effectively torpedo the Chancellor's policy of curbing inflation by curbing pay increases. When, and if, the proposed national rent rebate scheme comes into effect the dilemma will be still more marked. The rebates will tighten the poverty trap — unless of course the tenants do not claim a means-tested housing allowance.

The present impasse should compel both the trade unions and the government to reconsider their attitudes towards low pay and family poverty. For the unions it is a great and novel opportunity. By demanding — and obtaining — as part of the next wage round a return to the principles of Beveridge they would increase the net pay of family men, concentrating help on those with family responsibilities who are in greatest need, lift most working families off means-tests and clear of the poverty line, and build a firm base from which minimum wage demands could be launched. If they seize their chance there is a real possibility that the lasting consequence of the Government's means-test madness will be an extension of universal social provision achieved through union strength. Over to you Jack Jones.

Killing a Commitment: the Cabinet *v* the Children (1976)

The scuttling of the commitment to child benefits is a case study in how cabinets decide major policy issues. It illustrates not only the ease with which a majority of the cabinet can be stampeded against a long-term commitment of the party, but also the way a Prime Minister and Chancellor can manipulate a situation to their own ends.

Within the space of two cabinet meetings in May, ministers decided to go against strong arguments which had been developed for a decade in favour of reforming financial support for children. In the mid-1960s Richard Titmuss called attention to the haphazard nature of child support in this country. Second and subsequent children only received family allowances. Differing rates of benefit were paid for children whose parents were drawing supplementary benefit and national insurance benefits. Parents in work were allowed to claim tax allowances for all children. But many parents on a low income did not earn enough to set the child tax allowances against their tax liability. So poverty groups began calling for a merging of the family allowance and child tax allowance system in the payment of a single uniform benefit.

This argument was reflected in the thinking of the Conservative Party. Miss Mervyn Pike (now Baroness Pike) advocated a simple form of negative income tax. Under this, parents who did not earn enough to claim their child tax allowances would gain the value of the allowances as a cash payment.

The debate on how best to give financial support for children got a Great Leap Forward with the publication of the Heath government's 'green paper' on tax credits. As part of the scheme, family allowances and child tax allowances were to be replaced by the payment of a uniform tax credit for children. The scheme entailed a double transference of income. The poorest families who were not claiming the full value of the child tax allowance would receive a net increase in family income. For many other families, the main effect of the proposal was to transfer income from husbands (who would lose their tax allowances) to wives (who would pick up the new payment at the post office).

Trade union leaders who appeared before the House of Commons select committee inquiring into the tax credit proposals, not only grasped the impact of the new measure in terms of distribution of income, but also were willing to sell the scheme to their rank and file. Looking back, one error made by the poverty lobby — the Child Poverty Action Group and others — was to assume that future cabinet ministers were as quick as trade union leaders in grasping the full significance of the reform.

Labour members on the select committee opposed the idea of tax credits. As part of an alternative package deal, the Labour Party proposed a new 'child endowment' scheme. This was later renamed 'child benefits'. The scheme was in essence exactly the same as the tax credit proposals as they applied to children.

A Child Benefit Bill duly reached the statute book on 7 August 1975. Some MPs moved an amendment to write into the bill the starting date for the full scheme. But the government said this was unnecessary because they had given a number of binding commitments.

There were indeed difficulties of the most down-to-earth kind. There were delays over the building intended to house the staff administering the benefits (at one time it was thought that the construction firm had used high-alumina cement). There were problems with the ordering of a computer, and with the recruitment and training of staff. Nevertheless, ministers gave a categorical assurance that the scheme would begin in April 1977. Privately, ministers have admitted that the scheme could have started a year earlier if the money had been available to pay a generous rate of benefit. Instead, the 'child interim benefit' was brought in in April 1976. The first child of single-parent families became eligible for a benefit of £1.50 a week.

The one remaining issue on which the cabinet had to decide was the rate at which full child benefit would be paid from April 1977. On 8 April this year, three days after Callaghan's election as Prime Minister, the reshuffled cabinet received a memorandum from the new Secretary of State for Social Services, David Ennals, who had that day taken over from Barbara Castle. This spelt out that families with children were now getting substantially less support than the Tories provided in 1970, 1971 and 1972, and less than the Labour government provided in the late 1960s. Further, the increase in child tax allowances announced in Healey's 6 April budget had done little more than restore family support to its 1974 level, which was still substantially below the provision in 1971. Ennals's memo concluded with the words: 'If we continue to let child support be eroded by inflation, the whole scheme would be condemned as a trick to give children less, not more.'

The Secretary of State's memorandum informed the cabinet that a child benefit of £2.90 was required to restore the support for a three-child family to the level it had been under the Tories in 1971. Dennis Healey, as Chancellor of the Exchequer, countered this proposal in a note of his own. The Treasury was thinking in terms of a child benefit of £2.50 a week plus 50p premium payments. These were to go to the children of single-parent families, and to those families with larger numbers of children.

The Treasury position was attacked in a further memorandum by the new Secretary of State which was issued for the cabinet meeting of 4 May. A £2.50 child benefit plus 50p premium would mean that almost all two-parent families with more than one child would be worse off in real terms by April 1977 than they are now. Again the memorandum hammered home the point that to spend less in real terms in 1977 on family support would surely be looked upon by many people as a confidence trick.

The cabinet minutes for 29 April record the Secretary of State as saying that failure to increase the real level of support for families would add to the difficulties in negotiating pay policy with the TUC, and would be likely to harden their resistance to the phasing out of food subsidies. It was at this cabinet meeting that members began to discuss the effects of withdrawing child tax allowances on the negotiations for stage three of incomes policy. The cabinet concluded that it might be best to postpone the child benefit if the funds were not available to pay an acceptable rate.

Sensing the danger, David Ennals outlined the obstacles to a postponement of the scheme at the following cabinet meeting, on 4 May. Some of the objections were administrative. For example, what was going to happen to the building and the staff who were now in post to administer the new scheme? Further, the government would be rightly accused of bad faith. The Department of Health and Social Security itself argued that £2.70 child benefit remained the lowest desirable rate, and £2.65 the lowest flat rate which would ensure that no family was made worse off in cash terms. The cost of a £2.65 child benefit was put at £160 millions a year, plus £45 millions for dependent children overseas.

At this 4 May meeting the cabinet also received a further note from the Chancellor of the Exchequer and a memo from Joel Barnett, the Chief Secretary to the Treasury. These reiterated the point that a basic rate of £2.45 plus 50p premium payment would give cash gains to all families and a real gain to families with one child and to one-parent families.

Dennis Healey added that there was no commitment to maintain the child benefits in line with inflation as had been assumed by the previous submission by David Ennals. Furthermore, as the Chancellor believed that only 7 per cent of families drawing family allowances were poor or hard-pressed, the use of premium payments was a more cost-effective way of tackling poverty.

After the 4 May cabinet meeting, the new Prime Minister began working behind the scenes. At the cabinet meeting of 6 May, he reported receiving an 'excellent report' from the Whips Office which had created fresh doubts in his own mind about the political implications of introducing child benefit. The new Chief Whip, Michael Cocks, reported to the cabinet that, after surveying opinion (though the minutes do not recall whose opinion was canvassed), the introduction in April 1977 of child benefit would have grave political consequences which had not been foreseen when the bill went through the House of Commons. In the ensuing discussions cabinet ministers expressed the belief that the distribution effects of child benefit could not be 'sold' to the public before this scheme was brought in in April 1977. In summing up, the Prime Minister commented that to defer the scheme would *also* require careful public presentation. The two cabinet meetings of 4 and 6 May had scuttled the child benefit policy.

Under the guise of how best to present publicly the immediate abandonment of introducing child benefits, DHSS officials later put forward a number of policy alternatives. Shirley Williams as Paymaster-General and Secretary of State for Prices and Consumer Protection, and David Ennals, argued in an attached memorandum for those proposals which were aimed at salvaging something for families. Their view was that the government would gain respect for introducing the child benefits scheme in a modest form rather than by making a U-turn on a major commitment on which the government had fought two general elections and had enshrined in subsequent legislation.

The cabinet discussed this on 20 May. But it was now having to make its decision on child benefit in the knowledge that much of the cabinet discussion was being leaked to two major national newspapers. As a result of these leaks, those trade union leaders who were committed to child benefit insisted on inserting the crucial phrase into the statement agreed by the TUC/Labour Party Liaison Committee at their meeting on the 24 May. The statement read: 'It is of the utmost importance that the new child benefit scheme, to be introduced next year, provides benefit generous enough to represent a determined and concerted attack on the problem [of poverty].'

The full trade union delegation at that meeting did not know that a small group of union leaders — those who lead the trade union side on the National Economic Development Council (Neddy) — had arranged to see the Chancellor of the Exchequer and other senior ministers later in the day. At the cabinet meeting on the following day (25 May), the Prime Minister asked the Chancellor to report on this meeting with TUC chiefs to discuss the proposals put forward at the cabinet meeting on 6 May. The TUC were asked to agree to a postponement of the child benefit scheme for three years because of the effect the loss of child tax allowances would have on take-home pay. The cabinet minutes record: 'On being informed of the reduction in take-home pay, which the child benefits scheme would involve, the TUC representatives had reacted immediately and violently against its implementation, irrespective of the level of benefits which would accompany the reduction in take-home pay.' Both TUC and cabinet ministers were agreed in opposing any cut in child tax allowances, on the ground that this would appear to reverse part of the budget strategy underlying stage two of the incomes policy.

In order to prevent any further leaks finding their way into the national press, the cabinet then proposed that the announcement on the effective postponement of child benefits scheme should be made in the House of Commons that afternoon. At 3.30 pm on 25 May, David Ennals therefore rose and made the best he could of the government's abandonment of its plan to tackle family poverty.

The child benefit fiasco raises some very important lessons on the way the cabinet makes and unmakes major decisions. It is quite clear from the cabinet minutes that no minister really understood the reasons for this major commitment. The effect on take-home pay *had always been the point*. One can only wonder on how many other issues this kind of confusion is also true. How can this occur?

The minutes give a clear idea of how the present cabinet views political activity. The Prime Minister was insistent on a careful sell for the U-turn on child benefits. It is a clear example of a potentially radical government becoming managers rather than reformers. No time was given over to how the *original* decision could be 'sold' to families between now and next April.

What would the Prime Minister's, the Chancellor's and their colleagues' reactions have been if they had known they were going to be individually accountable for more open government? After all this is another of Labour's election pledges.

8 The Minimum Needs of Children

This paper was first presented to the Statistical Section of the Royal Statistical Society in 1978. It details how the relative needs of children were inaccurately calculated from the first definition of poverty established by Rowntree in 1899. This information became a constantly recurring theme in the Group's campaigns and has helped to build up support for the idea of a family lobby, being extensively used in the Group's campaigns leading up to the 1979 Budget (see, for example, 'Priority for all Children', CPAG, 1978). The essay also looks at how poverty was defined in relative terms by Booth and, apart from his first exercise, in similar terms by Rowntree. The emphasis on the relative definition of poverty in the post-war period is now working against the interests of the poor. Some politicians have willingly misunderstood the position, arguing that the poor exist only because poverty is defined in relative terms.

Introduction

This paper touches on four related themes. The first looks at how poverty has been defined by researchers in this country. It will show that, with one exception, poverty has invariably been described in relative terms. However, the second stage of the argument will show that campaigners and researchers have, possibly for political reasons, presented their findings on the poverty line in subsistence terms. A third theme will try and show how the researchers' presentation of a subsistence level has much influenced the public's attitude to what it believes is a proper standard of living for the poor. Finally, the paper examines the present situation where the public is hostile to the poor's present standard of living even though there is growing evidence that we should be embarking on a re-definition of poverty more appropriate to the 1980s.

The first definitions of poverty

Charles Booth

Of Booth's contribution to the social sciences, his biographers, the Simeys, have written that his

> most striking innovation was his invention of the Poverty line and his exploration of the methods whereby this might be established... His definition of poverty was perhaps the first operational definition in the social sciences, 'operational' in the sense that it provided the means whereby the truth or falsehood of his provisional hypothesis could be tested experimentally.(1)

Impressive as this development was, it by no means amounted to the sum of Booth's achievements. His attempt to reject what he regarded as Hyndman's and the Social Democratic Federation's irresponsible claim that as many as 25 per cent of the population of London were living in conditions of extreme poverty resulted in the application of survey techniques to social problems, the findings of which were also used to change and develop social policy.(2) Booth set out his definition of poverty in the second paper he read to the Royal Statistical Society in 1887, a paper which also contained the preliminary results of his London survey. He informed his audience that

> By the word 'poor', I mean to describe those who have a fairly regular though bare income, such as eighteen shillings or twenty shillings per week for a *moderate* family, and by 'very poor', those who fall below this standard, whether from chronic irregularity of work, sickness, or a large number of young children. I do not here introduce any moral question: whatever the cause, those whose means prove to be barely sufficient, or quite insufficient for decent independent life, are counted as 'poor' or 'very poor' respectively: and as it is not always possible to ascertain the *exact* income, the classification is also based on the appearance of the home.(3)

So we see that phrases such as the poverty line, at and below the poverty line, were used in this paper which was the first to report his poverty findings. The Simeys concluded that, 'Booth never achieved a clear definition of "poverty"'.(4) Other researchers, with Booth doing little to disabuse them, assumed that he had given a much more precise definition than a careful reading of his works could justify. Booth never laid down an explicit money level of income at or below which people should be considered poor, nor was any shape or form given to what was meant by a 'moderate' family.

In a paper to the Society in the following year, Booth made it plain that he was not seeking a 'scientific' definition of poverty. The classification of those who were poor and very poor was determined by popular opinion as expressed by his interviewers who had the job of classifying families. That poverty was a relative concept for Booth can be seen from a key passage in his second paper. Families are defined as 'very poor' when their means are insufficient 'according to the usual standard of life in this country'.(5)

Seebohm Rowntree

The source of the belief that poverty could be defined almost independently of the society in which the investigation was being carried out is to be found in Seebohm Rowntree's work. That he adopted this approach owes something to the political circumstances in which he was operating. Rowntree faced a different task to Booth. As do so many of today's campaigners, Rowntree felt the need to counter any charge that his findings might exaggerate the extent of poverty; hence his constant emphasis on a minimum subsistence approach. Writing at the beginning of his first report, Rowntree recalled that, 'Before we can arrive at an estimate of the number of those who are living in 'primary' poverty in York, we must ascertain what income is required by families of different sizes to provide the minimum food, clothing, and shelter needful for the maintenance of merely physical health.' He went on to add, 'Expenditure needful for the maintenance of mental, moral and social sides of human nature will not be taken into account at this stage of the enquiry. Nor in thus estimating the poverty line will any account be taken of the expenditure for sick clubs or social insurance. We confine our attention at present simply to an estimate of *minimum necessary expenditure for the maintenance of merely physical health*.'(6)

Food. There were three components in Rowntree's poverty line; food, rent and household sundries. He calculated the minimum food requirement in four stages; by looking at the function of food in the body, the quantity necessary to fulfil these functions, its kind, and its cost. To answer the technical side of these questions, Rowntree relied heavily on the work of Professor W. O. Atwater, who worked in the United States Department of Agriculture. Commenting on this choice, Asa Briggs has written that it was 'a good one, for Atwater, whose research on energy and nutrition marked a landmark in the history of nutritional science, had carried his studies to the point where they could be directly related to social investigation.'(7) Rowntree also relied on Atwater's work when calculating the dietary requirements of people of different age and sex. These differences were expressed as a fraction of the food required by an adult man. Later we will question how accurately these ratios reflected the needs of children, particularly in adolescence. Rowntree depended on Atwater in another respect. He chose the Atwater dietary scale for those men engaged on *moderate* muscular work — 3,500 calories of energy value and 125 grams of protein per man day. Commenting on this choice, Rowntree recalled, 'In selecting this standard, it must be borne in mind that the section of wage-earners living near the poverty line is composed mainly of labourers, to whom the bulk of the *heavy* work is allocated. Their wives have much *hard* work in washing and scrubbing. Their children also go to work young, and both during school days and afterwards, they often have to help at the home in scrubbing floors, running errands, etc. Thus, their young lives are *hard* and the hours during which they are working . . . are often long' (italics added). And, again never losing the opportunity to emphasise the stringent basis for his calculations, Rowntree added, 'In view of these facts, it is evident that whatever objection may be taken to the standard of food requirements here adopted, it cannot be said that the standard is too high.'(8)

Rowntree's next decision concerned the kind of food which would fulfil the dietary requirements. 'To this end, valuable suggestions may be gained from the diets provided for able-bodied paupers in workhouses, as the object in these institutions is to provide diet containing the necessary nutrients at the lowest cost compatible with a certain amount of variety.'(9) New guidelines on standard diets for the workhouse had come into force in March, 1901. In making selections, the guardians had certain instructions to follow, e.g. that they were to provide not fewer than two boiled or roast meat dinners a week.

Rowntree selected a diet from the ration specified in the new regulations 'but the cheapest rations only have been chosen, and on this account, no butcher's meat is included in the dietary. *The standard here adopted is, therefore, less generous than that which would be required by the Local Government Board*' (who were responsible for running the workhouses). Rowntree costed this diet based on the average prices paid for food by a sample of working class families in York, ignoring their findings only when prices were lower at the local Co-operative Stores. As a result of these calculations, Rowntree was able to detail the costs of the standard diet for families of different size according to the age of their children. The cost of feeding an adult was put at 3s while the cost for children ranged from 2s 1d a week for children under three to 2s 7d for children aged between eight and sixteen. However, in his final calculations, Rowntree took an average cost for a child's diet of 2s 3d a week and so, from its inception, this first detailed calculation of poverty was weighted against families with older children.

Rowntree added an important qualification to his figures. 'These prices refer solely to the cost of food materials: they include none of the necessary expenses connected with cooking. It must also be remembered that at the present, the poor do not possess knowledge which would enable them to select diet that is at once as nutritious and as economical as that which is here adopted as the standard. Moreover, the adoption of such a diet would require considerable changes in established customs, and many prejudices that would have to be uprooted.'(10) In other words Rowntree was asserting that although his dietary standards constituted the minimum requirement they represented an unachievable goal for many of the poor.

Rent. Rowntree then turned his attention to calculating minimum rent and household sundry costs. In estimating the necessary minimum expenditure for rent, Rowntree would 'have preferred to take some reliable standard of the accommodation required to maintain families of different sizes in health, and then to take as the minimum expenditure the average cost in York of such accommodation.' But he was forced to conclude that, 'This course would, however, have assumed that every family could obtain the needful minimum accommodation, which is far from the case.'(11) In all his minimum income calculations, Rowntree therefore took the actual rents paid 'as the necessary minimum rent expenditure.'(12)

Household sundries. The third component of Rowntree's poverty line income concerned household sundries, principal items consisting of boots, clothes and fuel. The estimates of the minimum expenditure on these items was based upon information gathered 'from a large number of working people.' Families were asked, 'What in your opinion is the very lowest sum upon which a man can keep himself in clothing for a year? The clothing must be adequate to keep the man in health, and should not be so shabby as to injure his chances of obtaining respectable employment. Apart from these two conditions, the clothing to be the most economical obtainable.'(13)

Information on the amount spent on clothing and fuel was collected without great difficulty, but data on the average sums required for other household necessaries 'proved very difficult to obtain.' Rowntree recalls that, 'Inquiries about this were usually answered by some such remark as; "if we have to buy anything extra, such as pots or pans, we have to spend less on food, that's all." ' In response, Rowntree added, 'it will not be overstating facts if we allow twopence per head to cover all household sundries other than clothes and fuel.'(14)

This then was the basis of Rowntree's minimum income which was consistent with 'merely physical efficiency'. Most of the criticism of Rowntree's approach has centred on the belief that his expenditure patterns consistent with gaining physical efficiency from a poverty line income were unrelated to the lifestyles of most working class families. Ironically this is true, but in the opposite way to that implied. Rowntree's attempt to produce a subsistence definition of poverty resulted in minimum income levels substantially above that obtained in reality by many working class families. The only person to notice this was Bowley who commented that, 'the food ration used by Mr Rowntree as a minimum is more liberal, so far as can be judged, than that obtained by the majority of the working class even in Europe in 1913, and by the great bulk of the unskilled and agricultural labourers in England before the end of the fall in prices in 1895. The human race has got along on a standard below this minimum, though it may have been hungry, with imperfect health, a high death rate, and a low standard of efficiency. It is very important to recognise this, for it has come as a surprise to many people to learn what a large proportion of even an advanced population is insufficiently fed . . . since they have not realised that the diet obtainable from wages of unskilled labour has in past times been generally too low for work of a high grade, and that the poor and the working classes were really interchangeable terms in past generations.'(15)

As we leave the examination of Rowntree's first attempt to define poverty, two issues in particular require emphasis. First, Rowntree's minimum income level guaranteed a standard of living in excess of that enjoyed by many working class families. And, second, at this time the poor and very large parts of the working class were but one body. We will comment later on the difficulties of pitching a minimum income level today which is in excess of the living standards of unskilled labourers, when many working class families have managed to distance themselves from poverty — if only by a few week's wage packets.

Revising poverty

After the completion of this first study of poverty in York, Rowntree returned on a number of occasions to the question of what constituted poverty. His first revisions were made in 1914 (although not published until after the end of the First World War). This study was characteristic of those which were to follow. Considerable emphasis was placed on the supposed scientific determination of minimum income and that this minimum was, if anything, set at an unbearably low level, while adjustments were made to the scale rates which ushered in the concept of relative poverty. Rowntree, like so many social reformers, found it necessary to dress radical findings in Tory clothes.

With his revisions to the poverty line in 1914, Rowntree begins to define poverty in the way Booth did — in setting minimum living standards that were current at the time of the study. And, while the 1914 revisions reduced the food requirements of the minimum diet, a new category of personal sundries was added. Commenting on this new entry, Rowntree observed that 'certain personal expenses . . . are quite necessary'. The items covered by personal sundries can be divided under three heads. First, a sum was included for compulsory National Health Insurance. Trade union subscriptions, or additional subscription to sick clubs, 'may almost be regarded as necessary, and this holds good of tram fares to and from work.' In addition, there are a number of other claims 'varying in their urgency — such as expenditure for newspapers, for incidental travelling, for recreation, for occasional presents to the children, for beer and tobacco, subscriptions to churches or chapel, burial and sick clubs for the wife and children, and the multitude of small sundries such as stamps, writing materials, hair cutting, drugs etc. — for which it is difficult to make an accurate estimate, but some outlay upon which it is impossible to avoid.' To cover all the items under the heading of personal sundries, Rowntree calculated, 'we cannot possibly allow a sum of less than five shillings a week' for a family of five.(16) Five shillings may seem little enough in today's money but it amounted to around 15 per cent of average earnings of manual male workers at the time.(17)

The items covered by personal sundries was extended by Rowntree in 1937 (the calculations for this second edition of *The Human Needs of Labour* was used as the basis for Rowntree's second poverty survey carried out in York in 1936). He added sums to cover the cost of a wireless, together with a holiday, books and travelling. But again, the dietary requirements were tightened, the protein level being reduced from 115 to 100 grams. Rowntree based this later change on the report of the advisory committee to the Ministry of Health which was published in 1931, maintaining that the findings of this committee were supported by the British Medical Association's own report (published in 1933) and the Technical Commission of the Health Committee of the League of Nations (which published its report in 1936).

Minimum subsistence in practice

The minimum subsistence levels were computed not only for the purpose of carrying out social surveys but also to influence public policy. Before the first World War Rowntree made his definition of poverty a relative one while at the same time emphasising its subsistence aspect, no doubt in an attempt to persuade the public to take seriously his findings on the extent of poverty. But we reach a catch-22 situation when these minimum subsistence income levels were recalculated by Beveridge.

In *Social Insurance and Allied Services* Beveridge laid the emphasis of the calculations squarely on the word minimum, though this was not a point emphasised in the report. As Beveridge's work got underway, politicians increasingly saw it as important in raising morale for the war effort. It was crucial that people had something better to look forward to after the cessation of hostilities. Hence Beveridge was able to write early on in his report that the 'determination of what is required for reasonable human subsistence is to some extent, a matter of judgement; estimates on this point change with time, and generally, in a progressive community, change upwards.'(18)

For his 1936 study, Rowntree updated his original primary poverty scale. Although some people in York were still living below this level in 1936, he also developed a human needs scale which, as we have seen, took into account changing perceptions of what people regarded as a decent standard of living, and this was a standard to which many working class people were able to aspire. Beveridge argued that the primary poverty scale would 'be rejected decisively by public opinion today', and he went on to assert that insurance benefits would have to guarantee a minimum standard of living related to Rowntree's human needs scale. However, a careful reading of the Beveridge proposals shows a minimum income level which was below the 1936 Rowntree standard.

The Beveridge Report

The aim of the Beveridge Report was to provide a system of insurance benefits which would prevent Want.(19) To do this, a claimant's individual needs would have to be met in full, including the payment of his rent. A number of experts argued with Beveridge that if Want was to be abolished, one condition of doing so was to pay claimants their actual rent in full. But, as Jose Harris records, 'Beveridge . . . was for once swayed by his official advisers — especially by the suggestion that a variable rent allowance would invest social insurance with the taint of a means-test.' Beveridge therefore, proposed a flat rate benefit which included a notional 10s for weekly rent and, as a result, 'he thus allowed himself to be stuck with the paradoxical proposition that benefits should be based on subsistence needs and yet should be uniform for all parts of the country.'(20)

Calculating a subsistence income. Apart from rent, Beveridge's subsistence level of income was made up of four component parts: food, clothing, fuel, light and sundries, together with a small allowance which he called the 'margin'. In working out the food component of a subsistence level income, Beveridge believed it was, 'possible to provide an adequate dietary', either on the scale laid down in the 1936 and 1938 reports of the Technical Commission on Nutrition by the League of Nations, or on the scale laid down in 1933 by the Committee on Nutrition of the BMA: At 1938 prices Beveridge costed the diet for a man and wife as about 13s a week.

In estimating the cost of clothing and of fuel, light, and sundries, Beveridge first reviewed the evidence on the level of expenditure from the Ministry of Labour family budgets. This survey of the expenditures of industrial households showed a husband and wife spending 4s 10½d a week on clothing in 1937–8. For agricultural households, the level was 3s 3d a week and, as Beveridge commented, 'These expenditures are above the subsistence requirement, since they relate to households which are living above the minimum.'(21) He therefore concluded, 'it is reasonable to put the allowance for clothing and unemployment disability benefit at 1s 6d for a man and a woman, or 3s 0d together'.

A similar exercise was carried out for fuel, light *and* sundries, and the recommended level for all three items was put at below the lowest expenditure recorded in industrial households for fuel and light consumption alone — 4s a week for a married couple.

Beveridge also made a small addition to the scale rates as 'Some margin must be allowed for inefficiency in purchasing (of food), and also for the certainty that people in receipt of the minimum income required for subsistence would, in fact, spend some of it on things not absolutely necessary.' This margin was set at 2s a week for a man and woman together and 1s 6d a week for a single person. How did this minimum standard compare with the human needs scale calculated by Rowntree in 1936?

Table 8.1 The Beveridge and Rowntree Human Needs Scale

	Rowntree (1936 prices)	*Beveridge† (1938 prices)*
Single man	22/9	12/6
Single woman	17/6	11/6
Man and Woman	27/8	22/-
Man & Woman + 1 child	33/-	29/-
Man & Woman + 2 children	38/4	36/-
Pension single man	15/3	11/6
single woman	12/6	11/4
couple	22/4	21/2

* This column is reproduced from Rowntree, B.S., *The Human Needs of Labour*, Longman, 1937.

† This column is reproduced from *Social Insurance and Allied Services*, HMSO, 1942

Comparison of Beveridge and Rowntree

The net result of these calculations was to draw up minimum income levels substantially below those proposed by Rowntree. The rate proposed by Beveridge for a single man and woman was 55 per cent and 66 per cent respectively of Rowntree's human needs scale. The rates for single pensioners range from 75 per cent and 91 per cent of the Rowntree rates for a single man and a single woman, to 95 per cent for a married couple. Beveridge's calculations for children were substantially more generous than Rowntree's although, as we shall see later on, it is questionable whether Beveridge's relativities were correct. Beveridge's minimum income level for a family with one child was 86 per cent of the Rowntree scale. For families with more than three children, the Beveridge scale was more generous.

Immense enthusiasm greeted the publication of *Social Insurance and Allied Services*, and 100,000 copies of the Beveridge Plan, as it became known, were quickly sold, in addition to the special cheap edition which was printed and distributed within the armed services.

One is left wondering whether there would have been such enthusiasm if the unsuspecting public had been aware of just how much less generous than Rowntree's 1936 standard was the proposal for minimum income levels in the post-war world; or, had it been known that the revision of Beveridge's scale rates would not have taken the war-time inflation fully into account. Beveridge's calculations were all based on 1938 prices. The cost of living rose by 73 per cent during the decade before the 1948 National Assistance Act was brought into operation, yet the minimum income scales were revised by only 56 per cent.

Minimum subsistence since Beveridge

Between 1948 and 1959, there were six revisions of the National Assistance Scale Rates which took account of changes in the cost of living. In June 1959, a White paper entitled *Improvements in National Assistance*(22) was presented to Parliament. This stated that the Government had been considering the position of those on National Assistance and had reached the conclusion that the time had come to move to a higher standard, so giving the poor a share in the increasing national prosperity.

To what extent have the 1948 subsistence levels been revised to take account of increasing national prosperity? There is no disputing the fact that the old National Assistance Scale, now the Supplementary Benefit Rates, have risen faster than the rising prices if we take the period since 1948, although, in the early years in particular, real cuts in living standards occurred during the period between reviews. From 1948, the scale rates have been revised by 80.8 per cent while price rises over the same period amount to 35.3 per cent (up till November 1975). The extent to which those on the minimum income level have gained an increasing share of rising national prosperity is more questionable if we measure the value of the scale rates as against average gross and net earnings.

Taking as our base line average gross earnings, we find that although 1959 does mark a closing of the gap between the living standards of those on benefit with children and those on average earnings, no marked improvement is recorded for single people or childless couples. Indeed, families on benefit gained only because of the withering away of family support for working families with children. Yet, taking the whole period, these gains were lost and, by 1977, the value of Supplementary Benefits expressed as a percentage of average earnings was very little different from when the National Assistance

Scheme was established in 1948.

A somewhat different picture emerges if the poverty line income for those on benefit is measured as against net earnings. Although the data do not show an appreciable improvement in relative living standards of the poor on benefit in 1959, despite Government statements to the contrary, taking the period as a whole, from 1948 to date, the current Supplementary Benefit Scale Rates are pitched at a significantly higher level of average net earnings than were the National Assistance Scale Rates in 1948.

A careful examination of the tables giving the National Assistance/Supplementary Benefit scale rates as a percentage of gross and net earnings suggests that any improvement in the relative living standards of the poor out-of-work has been brought about by the effects of taxation on the working poor rather than a deliberate Government policy to revise minimum income levels in line with rising national prosperity. It is with the speeding up of the fall in the tax threshold, accompanied as this move was by a growing proportion of average earnings being lost in taxation, that we see an improvement in the relative living standards of the poor on benefit. The periods most marked by a rise in the value of supplementary benefit measured against net earnings, or an increase in personal taxation, call it what you will, have coincided with Labour Governments. One example will suffice to illustrate this. The value of the single person's scale rate stood at 32.1 per cent of average net earnings in 1964. This rose to 37 per cent in 1970. When the Labour Party was again returned in 1974, it had fallen in value to 34.6 per cent. By 1977, it had again risen to 38.1 per cent. It would be fair to add, of course, that this analysis of the increasing burden of taxation takes no account of the 'social wage' gains of increased taxation.

Life at the bottom

We have already noted how the Attlee Government did not compensate fully for price rises when the Beveridge minimum income levels were translated into benefit rates in 1948. This move resulted in a cut in the real value of what was proposed as the minimum subsistence level for beneficiaries. But at the same time a further revision took place which counted against households with children. Beveridge set the rate for children at 58 per cent of the single person's rate. This relativity was not maintained in the National Assistance Board Scale Rates in 1948. Although the benefits for children were age-related, their average value was less than 44 per cent of the single person's rate. A child had to be aged over sixteen for the relative value of its benefit to be greater than that advocated by Beveridge in his flat rate proposal. These cuts in the scale rates for children were made, even though there was growing evidence at the time when Rowntree and Beveridge undertook their calculations that they had underestimated the relative needs of children.

By far and away the most important item in computing a minimum income level for children in both Rowntree's and Beveridge's work was the cost of food, and there are two major criticisms of the way in which they went about their calculations. First, although Rowntree wrote as late as 1950 that his food ratio was based on Cathcart's and Murray's tables, 'which are now generally accepted', these very ratios were already being challenged two decades earlier.(23) For example, the work of Gephart and Emmett Holt showed the food needs of adolescent boys as greater than that of the adult male. Similarly, the needs of adolescent girls were shown to be significantly greater than those laid down by Cathcart and Murray.(24)

The second criticism was double-barrelled. In his 1937 report, the Chief Medical Officer of the Ministry of Health drew attention to the fact that recent work had shown that a twelve to fourteen year old required about 90 grams of protein a day whereas the needs in an adult male were in the region of 70 grams. This ranked a child's requirements as 1.3 times those of an adult.(25) The Cathcart and Murray scale, on the other hand, placed a child's needs in this age group as 0.9 of a man's. On top of this, M'Gonigle and Kirby had written as early as 1936 that difference in diet costs between children and adults could not be made on straight ratio basis. This was because the protein requirements were different, with children needing more expensive protein.(26)

Evidence from two sources

If we leave aside the question on how adequately the basic rate of supplementary benefit has been revised to take account of the rise in national prosperity, there are two sources of evidence which show that the present scale rates for households with children severely underrate the relative needs of this group of the population. The first set of evidence comes from official surveys on the relative living standards of households on benefit. The second source of data comes from nutritionalists.

Official surveys. The official survey on the sick and disabled in (1972) and unemployed beneficiaries (1974) examined whether claimants had clothing which had brought their stocks up to the level laid down in Form BO/40 — the official guide to supplementary benefit officers making exceptional needs payments for clothing. Both surveys showed that households with children were less likely to own clothing stocks equal to the minimum rates. Forty-three per cent of single sick/disabled claimants without children had stocks of clothing less than the BO/40 level, but this rose to 61 per cent of claimants with two or more children. The equivalent figures for unemployed claimants were 49 per cent and 76 per cent respectively.

The surveys also reported on claimants who had fallen into debt since being on benefits. Again there was a close correlation between borrowing and the presence of children in the household. The surveys also showed that the additional cash from borrowing was spent on food, clothing, heating and housing costs. Reporting on the economies families had to make on benefit, as well as the extent of unmet needs, the official surveys concluded that, 'the claimants with families were . . . by several standards apparently more hard put to it than other claimants to balance their weekly budget. Some more subjective information gathered from the unemployed men also indicates that family men were the most hard pressed: the proportion of claimants who said they had cut down on their usual expenditure since being on benefit was highest (93 per cent) for family men.' The unemployed men were also asked whether, in spite of cutting down, borrowing and using savings, they still felt there was something they really needed and for which they were unable to find the money. The proportion who said that they had unmet needs increased steadily with family size, from 59 per cent of lone claimants to 89 per cent of those with three or more children. 'The family men were more likely to say they had unmet needs the longer they had been on benefit'.(27)

The Supplementary Benefits Commission drew upon these official surveys in its evidence to the Royal Commission on the Distribution of Income and Wealth to comment on the adequacy of Supplementary Benefit Scale Rates. Its conclusion stated that 'The evidence presented . . . regarding the standards of living of supplementary benefit recipients strongly suggests that the supplementary benefit scheme provides, particularly for families with children, incomes that are barely adequate to meet their needs at a level that is consistent with the normal participation in the life of a relatively wealthy society in which they live'.(28)

The evidence of nutritionalists. The second set of evidence about the adequacy of the children's rates in supplementary benefit is provided by nutritionalists. There have been two recent pieces of research which have attempted to calculate the adequacy of the food component of children's supplementary benefit rates.

The first was carried out by Michael Church in September 1975. He took the Supplementary Benefit Scale Rates for children aged between five and eleven and assumed that 75 per cent of this would be spent on food — it is important to recall that people living on average earnings spend about a third of their income on food. His next move was to take the DHSS's recommended intakes of nutrients for the UK, and those were applied over the age band from five to eleven for the largest and smallest of children. The final stage was to work out the cost of providing energy for these different groups of children. Once this exercise was completed, Church reported, 'only the most efficient mothers (at shopping), with the smallest children, could even hope to provide enough energy for their children on the allowance.'(29)

A similar, but more detailed analysis was carried out by Caroline Walker and Michael Church a year later. Data were taken from the 1975 National Food Survey on the food purchases of different socio-economic groups. The total energy value of the food consumed and its monetary value were then used to calculate the number of calories obtained per penny. This data was then updated for October 1976. This work enabled Walker and Church to challenge one very widespread belief about the consumption pattern of the poor. Contrary to popular prejudice, their results showed that, 'low income groups and large families tend to buy more efficiently than high income groups and small families'. Their second finding was based on spending the *whole* of the supplementary benefit allowance (for a five to ten year old) on food, which again showed, 'that the present supplementary benefit allowance . . . is inadequate to cover the food needs of the largest eight to ten year olds, even with the most efficient purchasing pattern'. And the authors added 'since the requirements of many five to ten year olds fall within the adult range, is it reasonable to pitch their allowance at only 33 per cent of an adult's?'(30)

Whatever dispute there may be about the extent to which those on benefit have shared in the nation's increasing prosperity, there can be little doubt that the minimum income level for children underestimates their real needs relative to adults. How true this is can be seen if we draw on the budgetary studies that have been undertaken since the end of the last century in Europe and the United States. These show that the cost of raising a child becomes equal to that of an adult at around the age of fourteen or fifteen. From then on, the needs of teenage children are seen to be greater than those of a single adult. This is not just because of the pressure of teenage culture. Dietary studies in the US have shown that the cost of feeding a thirteen to fifteen year old male teenager is 106 per cent of the adult rate, rising to 125 per cent for a male teenager between sixteen and nineteen. But it is when the total needs of children are taken into account, covering their clothing, personal care and recreation, as well as food, that one sees the full costs of maintaining dependants. The latest estimates given by the Community Council of Greater New York gives the following picture (Table 8.2).

Table 8.2 Total costs of food, goods and services: weekly basis, including clothing and household costs other than rent and utilities

	$	%
Dependent Adult(a)	30.50	100
Children(b)		
Under 1	10.80	32.88
1- 5	14.95	45.51
6-11	22.55	68.65
12-15	30.50	92.85
16-19	36.80	112.02

Source: *Community Council of Greater New York (1974) Annual Price Survey*, 18th Edition. This is a revision of their Family Budget Standard 1970, p. 22, Table IV. Data reworked by Margaret and Arthur Wynn.

(a) This adult is not working and not a head of household. To worker's total costs must be added the cost of working and to the householder's cost those expenses which he meets for household maintenance. The above relativities are the 'within the home' costs.

(b) The source gives costs for males and females separately at all ages but the differences are small. The figures given here are for males.

Here we see that the relative costs of a child under one are put at a fraction under 33 per cent of the adult rate, but this rises to almost 93 per cent for a twelve to fifteen year old child and to over 112 per cent for a sixteen to nineteen year old teenager. In comparison the SB minimum income levels are 17 per cent of the adult rate for children under five and 38 per cent for sixteen to seventeen year olds.

Conclusion

At about the same time as the Government was carrying out its own surveys on the living standards of sick and unemployed claimants, CPAG asked 60 families on benefit whom it had recently helped, if they would provide further information about what life is like for families dependent on benefit. From this information on their income and expenditure, a deprivation index was constructed, based on activities and customs which are common to the majority of the population. The index had seven component parts which were:

1 missing school because lack of suitable clothes or shoes;
2 never having a cooked breakfast (scored only when breakfast was missed through lack of money);
3 going all day without a cooked meal from getting up to going to bed;
4 not having a holiday in the past year;
5 inadequate footwear for when it rained;
6 going to bed early because of lack of fuel;
7 buying second hand clothes or clothes from jumble sales.

The results of this survey showed that 1 in 5 of the children in the sample was deprived in each aspect of life, measured by the index, and four-fifths of the children were deprived in at least four of the ways in which deprivation was defined for this exercise. It must be emphasised that the index was by no means exhaustive, for it excluded many other activities which could legitimately find a place, for example, never having an evening out, gaining the occasional treat, having birthday parties or spending extra money at Christmas. Nevertheless, it does give some indication about the cumulative nature of deprivation for some families on supplementary benefit.(31)

Yet public attitudes to what life should be like at the bottom appear to be firmly governed by Rowntree's subsistence approach. Recently, one of the public opinion polls asked a random sample which groups had done best over the past couple of years. *The Sun* newspaper reporting the findings commented on 'A high tide of resentment . . . flowing powerfully against a trio of groups . . . civil servants, trade unionists and the unemployed.' *The Sun* went on to talk about a national envy list with 85 per cent of respondents believing that the unemployed had done well in 1976.

Unfortunately there are not any other public opinion polls which give a national picture on the public's hostility to welfare. But there are many signs that the tide is running strongly against the poor. One example is the credence given to the stories about welfare abuse. Other examples of the backlash can be seen from CPAG's postbag. Firmly in the public mind is the impropriety of allowing the poor anything more than a subsistence income. 'Why should they have television?' or 'They don't need new clothes', are regular responses. Reports describing present living standards are greeted with 'write-ins' of useful recipes stressing the nutritional values to the poor of fish heads and the like.

Combating public hostility

The extensive public hostility to revising what is meant by poverty for the 1980s needs to be met in a number of ways. I end by touching briefly on two of these. In the first place, public discussion must start on how best to improve the living standards of those who earn their poverty. There are a number of ways of measuring the low paid. One is to look at the numbers who earn less than what they would be entitled to if they were not working and drawing supplementary benefits. In 1974, there were 130,000 wage earners earning less than the supplementary benefit level. A year later, the latest available data, their numbers had risen to 210,000.

Also in 1974, the TUC set a minimum wage target of two-thirds average earnings. In April 1977, the latest new earnings survey figures, there were 3.8 million workers earning less than this sum, even if we include overtime in the gross earnings figures. To combat low pay on such an extensive front, increases in benefits, particularly child benefits, have only a part to play. Serious discussion must also begin on the feasibility of implementing a national minimum wage.

The second approach to revising public attitudes to what is an acceptable minimum income in our present society could come from the commissioning of household budgetary studies. The irony is that whereas in this country emphasis was placed on defining poverty and carrying out social surveys on the extent of poverty, in the hope of mobilising public opinion behind welfare changes, European and American academics and reformers were concerned from the beginning of the century, and sometimes before, in building up details about the standards of living afforded for different households at given levels of income. Earlier, we drew on the budgetary study computed by the Community Council of Greater New York. We are almost the only Western country which has yet to begin a similar continuous exercise, and its commencement is long overdue.

9 Penalising All Children: A Study of Fiscal and Social Security Policy

'Penalising All Children', first presented to the Annual Meeting of the Public Administration Association in 1978, marks another stage in the move from a poverty to a family lobby. The paper examines the four forces – prices, taxes, family allowances, and eligibility to means-tested benefits – which have put families at a disadvantage compared to other groups in the population. By illustrating common interests, the aim of the poverty lobby was to exploit the sharp elbows of the middle class in support of policies which helped all families. How the relative living standards of families with children has deteriorated over the period since 1962 formed a crucial part in the Group's 1978 pre-budget submission 'Children Worse Off Under Labour'?

In opposing the Conservative Government's 1962 immigration restrictions Hugh Gaitskell commented that one could tell how civilised a country was by the way it treated its blacks. It would be equally true to say the the index of a country's confidence about itself can be measured in its approach to children. In this paper I will show that Britain's loss of confidence has coincided with an increasing penalisation of the family both in our tax and social security arrangements. The first section is concerned with how accurately we measure the individual needs of children in relation to adults. The evidence suggests that from the word go we have underestimated, often to a considerable extent, the costs of children. If this is true then we may have not only underestimated the numbers of poor but certainly underestimated the extent of hardship suffered by families. These two issues are examined in the paper's second section. Discussion then turns to recent post war policies which have penalised the family. In particular an examination is made of tax changes, eligibility for means-tested assistance and the failure to develop a generous system of child benefits. An attempt is then made to compare the disposable income of different persons and households since the early 1960s, before beginning a discussion on how best to redress the balance towards families.

Calculating need

A few years ago Professor Atkinson presented a paper to this conference entitled 'Income Distribution and Social Change Revisited'.(1) In doing so he not only updated some of the major Titmuss findings on the distribution of income, but began an evaluation of those forces which Titmuss described as countervailing the supposed trends to greater equality in income. In similar vein an alternative title for this paper would be 'Family Policy Revisited'. Those of you who are acquainted with the work of Margaret Wynn will know that I will be relying very heavily on the work of this remarkable person in the first part of the paper. That the relative living standards of families are now emerging as a political issue is due to her work and that of Della Nevitt. Margaret Wynn has a Beatrice Webb like intelligence and persistence without any of that dreadful snobbishness which is still to be found in some quarters of the Labour Movement. It was she who drew attention to the simple but rather important point that children are unevenly distributed amongst the population, with a small minority of adults being responsible at any one time for raising the next generation. At the present time three-quarters of all dependent children are in 22 per cent of households. Put another way, over half of all dependent children are in less than 13 per cent of households. This is not because of the preponderance of large families. Indeed, the average family size has so changed in recent years that the DHSS now categorises families with three or more children as being large families. Rather, rising living standards, the changing role of women in our society, the decline in national morale, as well as the numbers of women of child-bearing age, have all played a part in reducing the size of the child population.

Because only a minority of households are responsible at any one time for the welfare of our children, it has been an unspoken assumption in both our tax and social security provisions that the costs of raising the next generation should be shared to some extent throughout the community. There are two ways of looking at spreading the cost of raising the next generation. There is a snapshot approach which examines the contribution of today's single people and childless couples to those with children. There is also a life-cycle concept which focuses on spreading the cost within the household over time so that todays parents contribute towards the cost of other people's children once their own have left home. Central to this spreading of costs between different households now, and within households over different stages of the life-cycle, has been the way we have defined need.

The pioneers of poverty analysis

The first attempt at any rigorous analysis was undertaken by Seebohn Rowntree. This was set out in *Poverty: A Study of Town Life*(2) and in greater detail in the first edition of *The Human Needs of Labour*.(3) There he measured the needs of adults and children in the following way. Rowntree fixed the relative food needs of children at three-tenths of an adult's requirement for a child up to the age of two, rising to six-tenths for children aged between ten and thirteen years. Boys aged between fourteen and sixteen years were rated as needing eight-tenths, and girls of a similar age seven-tenths of an adult's food requirements. The clothing needs of all children, irrespective of their age, were set at three-quarters of the woman's rate and three-sevenths of the man's — or 9p per child. And while family budgets allowed for sundry items listed at 5s a week for a five-person family, this did not cover the specific needs of children.(4)

Rowntree returned to these calculations in the 1930s and by then we can see that he made the food requirements more generous for all children under thirteen years compared with those allowed in 1918, but they were still set at below the adult requirement levels. The relative clothing needs of children were likewise made slightly more generous but only compared to the needs of an adult man, and once again the small weekly sum of 9s for sundries did not cover any specific needs of the younger members of the household.(5)

It was on this revised Rowntree scale that Beveridge began his calculations which were to underpin *Social Insurance and Allied Services*. In this Beveridge remarked 'The Plan for Social Security starts with consideration of the people and of their needs.'(6) But what conclusion did Beveridge come to about the relative needs of children of different ages in relation to adults?

In setting the dietary requirements of children, Beveridge drew on the suggested intake laid down by the League of Nations. This set the requirements of children aged between ten and fourteen at 7s a week, a shilling more than for women and equal to the food allowance for men in Beveridge's assistance scales. In addition he advocated that the child's benefit should include a flat rate element for clothing and an additional small contribution towards the family's fuel costs. Children aged between fourteen and fifteen were allowed 7s 6d a week. But although Beveridge advocated that benefits paid to children should be age-related, his final figures gave an average of 7s for children, excluding their share of the rent. This amounted to a little over 58 per cent of the single person's rate.(7) This relativity was not maintained in the National Assistance Board's scale rates in 1948. Although the benefits for children were age-related, their average value was less than 44 per cent of the single person's rate. Indeed a child had to be aged over sixteen for the relative value of the benefit to be greater than that advocated by Beveridge in his flat rate proposal.

For once one must therefore take issue with Margaret Wynn when she comments that the Beveridge report was 'not based upon any serious analysis of the effects of age on the subsistence requirements of children and young persons. The conclusions about children's needs of the Beveridge report are, indeed, no longer tenable in the light of research taken during the twenty-five years that have passed since this publication.(8) We have already quoted evidence to show that Beveridge was much more aware than policy makers are today of the relative need of children and particularly teenagers. Where we can agree with Margaret Wynn is that more recent research suggests that even Beveridge underestimated some aspects of children's needs.

Drawing on Budgetary studies begun during the last century in Europe and the United States, it can be seen that the cost of raising a child becomes equal to that of an adult at around the age of fourteen or fifteen. From then on the needs of teenage children are seen to be greater than those of the single adult. (For fuller details see previous chapter).

These relativities can be compared with those laid down for children in the SBC scale rates. Sir Keith Joseph was known to have been impressed by the argument in *Family Policy* and this was reflected in the additional weighting to thirteen to fifteen year old children in the 1971 uprating. But even so the SBC relativities come nowhere near to those laid down by the Community Council of Greater New York. Indeed, some are barely half that suggested by the Council as adequate. The position is even less favourable for children if we take the long-term rates which are only awarded to adult claimants.

That our social policy to children does not reflect rationally their relative needs is also illustrated by the arbitrary changes in the value of child tax allowances. In 1957/8 the value of the child tax allowance for a child over sixteen was 107.1 per cent of the single person's tax allowance. By 1976/7 this had fallen to 49.6 per cent — a figure which excludes the effect of the claw-back arrangements introduced in 1968/9.

Underestimating children

Other important considerations stem from this information about the relative cost of children. Although we will not be able to say with certainty what the actual cost of children in relation to adults is in this country until we undertake budgetary studies similar to those carried out in most European countries and North America, we can say with very little fear of correction that our allowances for children in social security benefits grossly underestimate their requirements. But we use the supplementary benefit scale rates to measure poverty. It follows that if the cash allowances for children are wrong in relation to other rates, then we will be underestimating the numbers of families, and particularly the numbers of children, in poverty. For example, at the present time (1976–7) the married couple's ordinary weekly scale rate amounts to £20.65. In addition there are rates varying from £3.60 for a child under five to £7.80 for teenagers between sixteen and eighteen years of age. Families are defined as poor if their income is at or below the ordinary supplementary benefit scale rate plus an addition for rent. It follows that if the scale rates took account of the full needs of children, the poverty line income for families would be raised considerably. The numbers of poor would therefore be increased and the face of poverty would change.

Despite using a measuring rod which underestimates the number of poor children, such a change has already been taking place. In 1948 for each household headed by a person of working age and drawing national assistance, as it was then called, there were 1.7 pensioner households in receipt of benefit. By August 1976 this ratio had fallen to 1.1 households. A clearer demonstration of the changing face of poverty can be seen if we look at the number of persons, as opposed to households, dependent on this minimum income. In 1958 the retired and their dependants accounted for 63 per cent of supplementary benefit recipients; 37 per cent of recipients were below retirement age. By 1975 the balance had shifted, those below retirement age and their dependants accounting for 56 per cent of supplementary benefit recipients; those over retirement age, 44 per cent.

An even more marked change in the distribution in the numbers of poor between those above and below retirement age can be seen by examining the FES data from 1972. In that year there were 1.2 pensioners for every one other person under pensionable age living on incomes below the supplementary benefit scale rate. By 1975 the position has been more than reversed and the most desperate poverty was heavily concentrated amongst families. For each pensioner below the scale rates, there were 1.7 other poor people. This is not to say, of course, that many pensioners are not eaking out their last days in the most miserable conditions and on an inadequate income. The point at issue is that the poverty amongst pensioners is now more than matched by an increasing number of other people being kicked down to the bottom of the income pile. In this context it is important to remember that the way we define poverty underestimates its extent amongst households with children. If the scale rates more adequately reflected the relative costs and needs of children, the numbers of poor families would be increased considerably.

The failure to reflect adequately the cost of children in both our social security benefits and in the tax system also leads to an underestimation of hardship suffered by families, particularly those with teenage children. One illustration of this can be drawn from the SBC's evidence to the Royal Commission on the Distribution of Income and Wealth. Citing evidence collected in a survey of the sick in 1972 and of the unemployed in 1974, the Commission concluded that 'The claimants with families were . . . by several standards apparently more hard put to it than other claimants to balance their weekly budget'. (For further details of these surveys see the previous chapter).

Penalising the family

The difference in living standards of those with children compared with the childless applies throughout most of the income scale. In addition four forces have been at work, some relating from the very beginning of the post-war period, but others more recently, reducing the relative living standards of families with children. These are examined in turn.

Taxation

Lately awareness has been growing of just what a powerful engine taxation is in creating poverty.(9) Likewise it has been equally

Table 9.1 Value of tax allowances expressed as a percentage of the single allowance

Year	Single allowance as percentage of married allowance	Child tax allowances as percentage of single allowance			
		All children	Children not over 11	Children over 11, not over 16	Children over 16
1938–39	55.6	60.0	—	—	—
1939–40	55.6	60.0	—	—	—
1940–41	58.8	50.0	—	—	—
1941–42	57.1	62.5	—	—	—
1942–43	57.1	62.5	—	—	—
1943–44	57.1	62.5	—	—	—
1944–45	57.1	62.5	—	—	—
1945–46	57.1	62.5	—	—	—
1946–47	61.1	45.5	—	—	—
1947–48	61.1	54.5	—	—	—
1948–49	61.1	54.5	—	—	—
1949–50	61.1	54.5	—	—	—
1950–51	61.1	54.5	—	—	—
1951–52	57.9	63.6	—	—	—
1952–53	57.1	70.8	—	—	—
1953–54	57.1	70.8	—	—	—
1954–55	57.1	70.8	—	—	—
1955–56	58.3	71.4	—	—	—
1956–57	58.3	71.4	—	—	—

1957–58	58.3	—	71.4	89.3	107.1
1958–59	58.3	—	71.4	89.3	107.1
1959–60	58.3	—	71.4	89.3	107.1
1960–61	58.3	—	71.4	89.3	107.1
1961–62	58.3	—	71.4	89.3	107.1
1962–63	58.3	—	71.4	89.3	107.1
1963–64	62.5	—	57.5	70.0	82.5
1964–65	62.5	—	57.5	70.0	82.5
1965–66	64.7	—	52.3	63.6	75.0
1966–67	64.7	—	52.3	63.6	75.0
1967–68	64.7	—	52.3	63.6	75.0
1968–69	64.7	—	52.3 (33.2)	63.6 (44.5)	75.0 (55.9)
1969–70	68.0	—	45.1 (28.6)	54.9 (38.4)	64.7 (48.2)
1970–71	69.9	—	35.4 (22.5)	43.1 (30.2)	50.7 (37.8)
1971–72	69.9	—	47.7 (34.8)	55.4 (42.5)	63.0 (50.1)
1972–73	76.7	—	33.7 (24.6)	39.1 (30.0)	44.5 (35.4)
1973–74	76.8	—	33.6 (23.5)	39.5 (29.4)	44.5 (34.4)
1974–75	72.3	—	38.4 (30.1)	44.0 (35.7)	48.8 (40.4)
1975–76	70.7	—	35.6 (27.9)	40.7 (33.0)	45.1 (37.4)
1976–77	67.7	—	40.8 (33.7)	45.6 (38.5)	49.6 (42.5)

Source: Hansard, 30 March 1977, Vol. 929, col. 167–8.
For the years prior to 1957–58 there was a single rate of allowance for all qualifying children; the three age bands in present use were introduced for 1957–58.
The figures in brackets show the percentages after allowing for clawback.

Table 9.2 Tax threshold, together with the SB and FIS eligibility levels

	Single person		Married couple		Married couple with 1 child		
	Tax threshold £ per week	Supplementary benefit level £ per week	Tax threshold £ per week	Supplementary benefit level £ per week	Tax threshold £ per week	FIS entitlement level £ per week	Supplementary benefit level £ per week
January 1970	6.31	7.11	9.29	10.76	12.12	—	12.28
January 1971	8.04	7.79	11.50	11.81	14.35	—	13.49
January 1972	8.04	8.33	11.50	12.52	15.35	18.00	14.31
January 1973	11.38	9.28	14.85	13.97	18.67	20.00	15.96
January 1974	11.44	10.69	14.90	15.15	18.75	21.50	17.29
January 1975	12.02	11.63	16.63	17.45	21.25	25.00	20.57
January 1976	12.98	15.69	18.37	23.67	22.98	31.50	27.27
January 1977	14.13	18.39	20.87	27.70	26.63	39.00	31.28

	Married couple with 2 children			Married couple with 3 children			Married couple with 4 children		
	Tax threshold £ per week	FIS entitlement level £ per week	Supplementary benefit level £ per week	Tax threshold £ per week	FIS entitlement level £ per week	Supplementary benefit level £ per week	Tax threshold £ per week	FIS entitlement level £ per week	Supplementary benefit level £ per week
January 1970	13.92	—	13.98	16.35	—	16.08	18.77	—	18.33
January 1971	16.15	—	15.39	18.58	—	17.34	21.00	—	19.49
January 1972	18.13	20.00	16.31	21.54	22.00	18.76	24.94	24.00	21.76
January 1973	21.46	22.00	18.21	24.88	24.00	20.96	28.27	26.00	24.36
January 1974	21.44	24.00	20.15	24.81	26.50	22.66	28.17	29.00	26.05
January 1975	24.87	28.00	23.83	29.13	31.00	27.13	33.44	34.00	30.95
January 1976	26.60	35.00	31.22	30.88	38.50	35.73	35.17	42.00	40.90
January 1977	31.40	43.50	35.99	36.85	48.00	41.32	42.29	52.50	47.38

Source: *Hansard*, 22 May 1977, Vol. 930, col. 182–4.

1. It has been assumed that the children are aged 4; 4 and 8; 4,8 and 11; and 4,8,11 and 15 respectively.
2. The tax thresholds relate to earned income.
3. The figures for supplementary benefit include an addition for rent and rates based on the estimated average amount allowed to an unemployed person in each family status and for each year; the estimate for January 1977 is provisional.

successful in shifting the burden of taxation from single people and childless couples onto the backs of those with children, irrespective of the level of income. That is not to say that the tax burden has not increased for all groups of the population, but this increase has been disproportionately placed on households with children. Such a trend can be seen if we examine the tax threshold for earned income for each year since the end of the Second World War and the value of the threshold at 1945 prices. Such an analysis shows that whereas the tax threshold for a single person has risen from an index of 100 in 1945/6 to 187 for the most recent financial year, 1976/7, the tax threshold for a two-child family has risen from 100 to only 114 and for a four-child family to 109.

The reason why the tax threshold for families has fallen faster than that for other taxpayers has been the declining relative value of child tax allowances. The value of child tax allowances in 1957/8 (when age-related allowances were introduced), as a proportion of the single person's allowance, stood at 71.4 per cent for children not over eleven, 89.3 per cent for children over eleven but not over sixteen, and 101.7 per cent for children over sixteen. By 1976/7 they had fallen to 40.8 per cent, 45.2 per cent and 49.6 per cent respectively of the single person's allowance, and these figures take no account of claw-back. Nor has this decline been uniform. For example, in 1970/1 the child tax allowance for the youngest child stood at 35.4 per cent of the single allowance. In the following year it had risen to 47.7 per cent, falling back to 33.7 per cent in 1972/3, a year later.

One consequence of increasing the relative tax burden of families with children has been to tax them even though their income is below the supplementary benefit or FIS levels. At no time has the tax threshold for a single person or married couple been below the supplementary benefit level. That is not so for families with children. By 1976 a married couple with children began to pay tax on an income less than the supplementary benefit poverty line. On the other hand, the tax threshold has been below the FIS entitlement level since the very inception of the scheme. This has itself been a crucial ingredient of the poverty trap.

Inflation

A second but more recent force affecting families has been the differential impact of inflation. In evidence to the Royal Commission on the Distribution of Income and Wealth the Low Pay Unit showed that over a considerable period of time the cost of necessities had tended to increase faster than the overall price level. Since low income groups as well as families devote a larger proportion of their budget to these items, the cost of living for the poorest households, and families, has risen more rapidly than that of households in general, while the cost of budgets of higher income groups, and those without children, has increased more slowly (see Chapter 6 for more details).

Failure of family support

The third force which is partly accountable for the relative decline in the living standards of families is our failure to develop a generous system of family support. Ruth Lister and her colleagues in the Child Benefits Now Campaign have recalled the failure on this front from the word go.

The principle of family allowances was accepted by the Government with the publication of the Beveridge report in 1942. The allowances for second and subsequent children were first paid in 1946. The exclusion of the first child was justified on the grounds that the wages system was adequate to support a man, wife and one child. But the payments in 1946 to eligible children were of 5s a week compared with 8s suggested by Beveridge four years previously. The 5s allowance, which was not age-related as suggested by Beveridge, was justified on the grounds that it would soon be backed up by the extension of free school meals and milk to all children. A system of free meals for all children has never been introduced and the benefits of free milk have been lost during the last ten years or so.

It can be seen, therefore, that from the very beginning, the system of cash support for families was inadequate. In 1942 family allowances were viewed as the 'basic social service payment for children'. By 1944 they were being viewed as merely making a 'general contribution' to the needs of children. In the years since 1948 pensions and other main benefits have been increased eighteen times. In contrast family allowances or, as they are now called, child benefits, have been increased only five times. Consequently, in 1948 the family allowance payment for a two-child family was valued at a little over 4 per cent of average earnings. By 1976 its value had fallen to 1 per cent of average earnings. It was this falling relative value of family support that the child benefit scheme was designed to reverse. But although the new benefit covers all children, and a £1 allowance is paid for the first child except for single-parent families where the allowance is £1.50, the relative value of child benefits for a two-child family stubbornly remains at 1 per cent of average earnings.

The fiasco over the implementation of child benefits has been recorded elsewhere.(10) The new benefit scheme became payable in April 1977 and resulted in an additional £94 million being paid to families with children. At the same time Denis Healey the Chancellor of the Exchequer introduced a budget which reduced taxation by £2¼ billion. Not one penny of this sum went specifically to households with children. Child benefit, which was meant to be the beginning of a new era of financial support to the family, is taking on the appearance of a Trojan horse. The Chancellor of the Exchequer argues that if he increased child tax allowances, this would ensure that support went to most working families, as practically all families now pay tax, while at the same time not increasing public expenditure. But child tax allowances have now in effect been frozen during the transitional stage of implementing child benefit. The alternative to increasing child tax allowances is a change in the level of child benefit. But the moneys spent on child benefit qualify for the label 'public expenditure'.

Means-tested benefits

A fourth discrimination against families is to be seen in eligibility for various means-tested benefits. The failure to implement fully the Beveridge National Insurance proposals, and to extend coverage to those groups originally excluded, has resulted in the growth of the means-tested welfare state. But the family has lost even under a programme which is often sold as concentrating resources on those in greatest need. This can be seen for example by looking at the eligibility for the rent and rate rebate scheme. The needs allowance — which measures the householder's family circumstances — is put at £23.05 for a single person and £32.75 for a married couple or a single parent. To this is added £5.35 for each dependent child — giving each child less than a 23 per cent relativity to a single person. And whereas £1.90 is added to the needs allowance if the tenant or spouse is blind or disabled, and registered with a local authority department, no such adjustment is made to the needs allowance for children to compensate for the extra expenses of such handicaps. The net effect therefore is for families with children to pay a higher proportion of their income in rent and rates than other groups in the population. A similar picture emerges if one examines the other major means-tests.

Poor children or all children?

One way of evaluating the effect of some of the forces undermining the relative position of households with children is to look at the disposable income of different households. After deducting indirect taxation but adding back food and housing subsidies and taking 1962 as equal to 100, it can be seen that the indexed disposable income of a single pensioner had risen by 1975 to 183 and a two-pensioner household to 179. The disposable income for a single person had risen over the same period of time to 152, in contrast to a rise of only 136 for a four-child family and 138 for a two-child family. This shows the extent to which families have lost out relative to other groups during much of the post-war period and particularly how smaller families have been most penalised.

These findings throw up a direct challenge to those in the poverty lobby who have been campaigning on behalf of children. The horizontal redistribution of income away from households with children has been happening over such a long time and is now so significant that one ought to question whether poor children would have been better served by a campaign centring on the needs of all children. We have only to look to our EEC partners to see how successful family lobbies can be. An examination of family allowance payments in the Common Market countries shows that only the Irish Republic pays less generous benefits than Britain — so much for family allowance payments encouraging large families! In contrast with a monthly payment of £4.66 for first children in this country, payments range from £7.02 in Italy to £12.16 in Germany, £12.80 in the Netherlands, £14.06 in Denmark, £15.74 in Luxembourg and £20.62 in Belgium. In the UK, second and subsequent children receive a monthly payment of £6.50. The second child in Belgium receives a monthly allowance of £32.72 while the fifth and subsequent children each receive monthly payments of £46.03.(11)

One reason for the difference in political muscle behind families in this country when contrasted with our European partners has been the strength of poverty studies in this country; a phenomenon almost unknown until recently in Europe. Ever since Booth's and Rowntree's studies on poverty at the turn of the century, there has been a continuous contribution to monitoring the living standards of the poor. Indeed, Beveridge in his post-war report on voluntary organisations listed the social survey, and its use in reporting on the condition of the people, as one of the most important functions of

Table 9.3 Indices of real income after taxes and transfers by household type 1962–1975 (a) (1962 = 100)

	1 adult pensioner(b)	*2 adult pensioners(b)*	*1 adult non-pensioner(c)*	*2 adult non-pensioners(c)*	*2 adults 2 children*	*2 adults 4 children*
1962	100	100	100	100	100	100
1963	102	110	118	105	109	103
1964	105	107	126	110	104	107
1965	115	114	121	108	102	108
1966	116	118	119	111	111	103
1967	125	122	126	112	110	108
1968	126	122	124	111	112	116
1969	134	124	122	114	116	122
1970	133	129	126	118	115	117
1971	135	124	127	121	121	127
1972	145	135	141	129	128	128
1973	162	157	146	140	135	148
1974	176	171	153	144	139	158
1975	183	179	152	143	132	138

Sources: *DHSS Abstract of Statistics for Index or Retail Prices, Average Earnings, Social Security Benefits and Contributions*, May 1980 (for prices)

Notes: (a) Disposable income less indirect taxes plus food and housing subsidies deflated by the retail price index (Disposable income = original income plust cash benefits less direct taxes).

(b) Pensioner households are defined as those where more than three-quarters of household income consists of National Insurance pensions and supplementary allowances to such pensions.

(c) Includes some retired households — see note (b).

the voluntary movement in this country.

And just as the poor in other EEC countries have been bereft of the attentions of social scientists for most of this century, the living standards of families have been protected and enhanced by strong family movements. Only in Britain could a Chancellor of the Exchequer announce budget concessions of £2¼ billion while at the same time devoting only £94 million to families, while at the same time planning to recoup more than this sum back from them in increased school dinner charges. The needs of the family are so much better recognised in the EEC countries that, even without the watch-dog function of families, Chancellors automatically respond to the needs of that minority of the population who are at any one time responsible for the next generation. But of course this is partly a chicken and egg situation. Governments are aware of the needs of families because of the effectiveness and forcefulness of family organisations.

Perhaps in the poverty lobby we have ignored for too long the beneficial effects which the sharp elbows of the middle class could have in getting the needs of families to the top of the political agenda. To mobilise this power on behalf of the poor we must begin to provide prizes for all families as opposed to just poor families. It is now in the interests of poor children that we develop a strong family lobby in this country. Of course there are dangers of trying to transplant organisations from one political culture to another. For example, the French family movement has massively strong grass-roots support. But a useful beginning could be made in establishing a public body charged with a watchdog function for the family, just as the National Consumer Council has been given responsibility for consumer interests. If such a body was made effective it would not only begin to permeate official thinking, but give that crucial lead to individuals at a grassroots level who at the present time feel isolated and berefit of leadership. The recent statements by Patrick Jenkin, the Opposition Spokesman on social services, calling for a central agency to promote the interests of families, show how far the Conservatives' thinking has already progressed in this respect. At the present time the only vocal organised support for the family comes from such quarters as the Festival of Light brigade. But as I hope I've shown, our real concern with the family's and thereby all our futures, should not only be with its moral well-being, but also with the powerful economic forces which have done so much during the post-war period to undermine the relative living standards of those with children.

10 Relating Family Income to its Needs

This edited version of a memorial lecture delivered in 1977 gives details of how the campaign was conducted immediately after the leak of Cabinet papers on child benefits in 1976. The Callaghan Government instituted major Civil Service and Special Branch enquiries in an attempt to find the leak. The paper recalls how I and Deep Throat, the name throughout the period of the person brave enough to leak the Cabinet papers, talked and corresponded after the publication in New Society of 'Killing a Commitment', so ensuring that Deep Throat was never identified. The way senior politicians and some trade unionists reacted to the child benefit scheme illustrates how deep is the prejudice against an issue which cuts across classes and transfers some economic power from men to women. Given the campaigning mistakes from the Family Endowment Society, these reactions are not dissimilar from the misgivings expressed by the Labour Movement in the 1920s and 1930s.

Today we remember again someone who was much concerned about the needs of children. Quetta Rabley worked here in the Southwark Social Services Department and was particularly concerned about the welfare of children, especially those brought into the care of the local authority. While research shows how important poverty is in determining which children spend part of their childhood under the aegis of a local authority, the recent Children Act (1975) clearly illustrates how the needs of children are discussed in a financial vacuum. The Act is the most significant piece of legislation affecting the rights of children for thirty years, and yet the financial needs and relative living standards of families with children went unmentioned.

We live in a country which likes to believe it looks favourably upon children. How then do we explain the paradox that it is the relative living standards of families with children which have shown the least advance during the past twenty years? Part of the answer stems from the nature of the campaign waged by reformers in favour of family allowances during the first forty years of this century.

Some of their arguments were bogus or open to misinterpretation, and children have paid the penalty ever since. But part of the answer is to be found in the peculiar circumstances by which the Family Allowance Act 1945 was heaved onto the statute book. In the first part of this paper I will examine these two forces a little more fully.

The discussion will then turn to what has become known as the child benefit leak and the way the cabinet managed to inflame old prejudices in the trade union movement to secure a scuttling of a major election manifesto commitment. We will see that one of the powerful arguments used by early reformers in favour of the introduction of family allowances had ironically prepared the ground only too well for the cabinet to make a quick U-turn on its commitment to families with children. The final section begins a restatement of the case for child benefits, after a two-decade period during which living standards of families have fallen relative to those of other groups who are not responsible for the welfare of children.

False prophets?

Without the campaigns conducted by Eleanor Rathbone it is doubtful whether the Family Allowance Act would have been passed in 1945, or any other year come to that.(1) But as we will see, our heroine was also responsible for using arguments in her campaign which, while at the time successful in getting the scheme of family allowances established, have been responsible for limiting the scope of the scheme in relating family income to its needs. Eleanor Rathbone was concerned to establish the principle that 'children should receive a little share of the national income given to them not in respect of their father's service in industry but in respect of their own value to the community as its future citizens and workers'.(2) In order to promote this idea Eleanor Rathbone wrote *The Disinherited Family*, which ranks as one of the most important books in the social sciences to be published during the first fifty years of this century.(3) In the preface to that book she commented that one of her main aims was to refute the idea that 'a living wage' could be the basis for determining a pattern of wages and salaries which would reflect family responsibilities. It is my contention that her success in achieving this objective goes a long way to explain the sub-conscious opposition of trade union leaders to the whole idea of family allowances and child benefits.

Today there is all too little reaction against the existence of whole industries and firms paying poverty wages. This has not always been so. In the years following the turn of the century a great deal of public concern was expressed at the existence of the sweated trades. The doctrine of 'a living wage' grew from the belief that the first call on industry was to pay a decent minimum wage to all workers. Campaigners for a living wage moved the argument on one step further by arguing that industry should pay a wage which allowed a man, his wife *and* his children to maintain a decent standard of living. It was this development of the concept of a living wage which Eleanor Rathbone attacked in two ways. In the first place she questioned the assumptions underlying a wage needed to support a man, his wife and his family. In his first study of poverty in York Rowntree calculated that over 15 per cent of the wage-earning class were living in primary poverty. Similarly, the survey carried out by Bowley in Northampton, Warrington, Stanley and Reading showed 16 per cent of working class households and 27 per cent of working class children living in primary poverty. Eleanor Rathbone noted that both these writers were prominent in the campaign for a living wage. Calculations for a living wage were based on the assumption of a family with three children. But, as she was quick to point out, had the living wage demands been granted, half of the children found to be in poverty would have remained so.(4)

The second criticism of a living wage stemmed from the question of whether society in those days had the resources to pay a minimum wage calculated on the basis of the needs of a three-child family. By quoting back to estimates made by Bowley himself, Eleanor Rathbone showed that if all income in 1911 above £160 a year were confiscated and redistributed to wage earners, 'This sum would have little more than sufficed to bring the wages of adult men and women up to a minimum of 35s 3d weekly for a man and 20s for a woman which Mr Rowntree in *The Human Needs of Labour*, estimates as reasonable.'(5) In other words, economic resources distributed in this way would guarantee an adequate minimum for men and women workers but the resources did not exist to cover the cost of children through the wage system. Thus the ground was cleared for Eleanor Rathbone to advocate relating family income to its needs by way of a national system of child allowances.

Trade union hostility and public misconception

In an age when trade unions spent so much of their time trying to resist wage cuts, let alone win wage increases, the campaigning arguments for family allowances could understandably be viewed as at best a diversion and at worst sabotage. That is not to say that there is anything in the writings of Eleanor Rathbone other than to support the notion that the first claim on industry was to pay decent wages. What she was at pains to point out, however, was that even if this was achieved, family income would not be related to family needs. That trade union leaders, and possibly more importantly, trade union rank and file, did not read the fine print on these statements is understandable enough. Too little effort was given over then, or more recently, to convince trade union leaders that the campaign was for both higher real wages and higher family benefits. As I shall recall shortly, failure to educate the trade unions on this complimentary policy made the government's scuttling of a full child benefits scheme that much easier to achieve.

A second boomerang effect came from the eagerness of campaigners to hijack the eugenics lobby to their cause. In Britain we become concerned about the size and quality of the population about every twenty or thirty years. By the 1930s, and particularly by the latter part of that decade, there was an increasing public concern about Britain's declining population. Reports showed that had those trends continued, the percentage of the population below the age of fifteen, which stood at 25 per cent in 1938, would have fallen to 7 per cent by 1975. Likewise, while 12 per cent of the population was over 60 in 1938, the projections showed a rise to 30 per cent by 1975. These projected changes in the age structure of the population were viewed with so much alarm that they swamped the Eugenics Society's arguments on encouraging births only amongst the upper classes.

The idea that family allowances were a measure to encourage people to have larger families was firmly cemented in the public mind by one of this century's great communicators. Churchill, as on so many occasions, brilliantly presented the need to take the right course of action, in this case on family support, for the wrong reasons. For example, in a war-time broadcast on the Beveridge scheme Churchill spoke in the following terms of the urgency for a national policy to give positive help to parents with children.

> One of the most sombre anxieties which beset those who look thirty or forty or fifty years ahead, and in this field one can see ahead only too clearly, is the dwindling birthrate. In thirty years, unless present trends alter, a smaller working and fighting population will have to support and protect nearly twice as many old people; in fifty years the position will be worse still. If this country is to keep its high place in the leadership of the

world and to survive as a great power, our people must be encouraged by every means to have larger families. For this reason well thought-out plans for helping parents to contribute this lifeblood to the community are of prime importance.(6)

Here then is the root of one of today's prejudices against adequate family benefits, namely, that they will encourage larger families. There is no evidence at all to support this view. But as is so often the case it is not what is, but what people believe to be true which is important. The dangers inherent in reformers using any argument to further their ends are only too plain to see.

Latent trade union hostility and public misconception about family allowances were not countered by a full and protracted parliamentary debate on proposed schemes. As Sir John Walley has recalled: 'Parliamentary and industrial, as well as academic, support for them (family allowances) had become so general by the time they came before parliament in the height of war, that they never got the popular understanding that normally comes from the political discussion of new and probably, therefore, controversial policies.'(7) Furthermore, the priority accorded to family allowances in the coalition government's post war planning 'also deprive them of any effective participation in the great publicity and educational drive to support those parts of the programme which fell to the Attlee Government to bring in; family allowances were already being paid as the first of these measures reached the statute book'.(8) Although given Churchill's and other Ministers' misconceptions about the schemes, this failure perhaps ought also to be viewed as a blessing in disguise.

Sir John has also noted that the assignment of ministerial responsibility for the new scheme did not add to public enlightenment. Beveridge viewed family allowances as part of the country's income structure. It would therefore have been more logical, as well as expedient, for the vote for family allowance moneys to remain with the Treasury. This becomes even more logical now that child tax allowances are being merged into a tax-free cash payment called child benefit. And just as Education Secretaries have been only too willing to sacrifice school milk and the school meals system in favour of safeguarding the more traditional aspects of the education budget, so too have the successive social security ministers been prepared to offer up family benefits on the altar of higher pensions and other related benefits. If family benefits had remained at the centre of the political stage

> their value would soon have been established in helping to untie the political as well as the financial knots into which post war national policy has got in such fields as housing subsidies and rent control, educational maintenance grants, income taxation and, above all, in the, so far, vain search for ways and means of controlling the inflation of wages, incomes and prices which now threatens to engulf us all.(9)

Child benefit leaks

When the Minister introduced family allowances he recalled that 'the baby is a very small one. We feel it will have to be a good deal fattened and cosseted before it reaches its proper stature.' But as Ruth Lister has noted, far from being fattened, family allowances were subjected to starvation.(10) In contrast, support given to families through the tax system took on a much more general form. For example, in the year during which the Government published the *Circumstances of Families*(11), itself the first ever official report on the extent of family poverty in Britain, the net value of family allowances for a four child family (two aged under and two over 11) was £39.50 a year while the net value of child tax allowances stood at three times this amount, at £163.20 a year. But child tax allowances were only of value to those parents paying income tax, and in 1967/8 a family with four children did not begin to pay tax until their income was almost at average earnings (in contrast to today when the Revenue expects a contribution when earnings reach around 60 per cent of average earnings). While all families gained help through the family allowance scheme for second and subsequent children, the system of child tax allowances was of no value to poorer families. Once poverty groups became aware of the extent of the inequalities in child support, they began calling for the abolition of child tax allowances, and for the revenue thereby saved to finance a new family benefit payable to all children.

The Green Paper

The Conservatives were the first political party officially to call attention to the inequities in child support. In the late sixties Miss Mervyn Pyke (now Baroness Pyke) advocated a simple form of negative income tax. Under this scheme parents who did not earn enough to claim their child tax allowances would gain the value of the child tax allowances as a cash payment. Over the next few years the Conservative Party revolutionised its ideas on social security and tax reform and the outcome of their deliberations was presented in the Heath Government's Green Paper on tax credits. Described by one academic as the most important proposal since the publication of the Beveridge Report, part of the scheme proposed the abolition of family allowances and child tax allowances, replacing them by a uniform tax credit for children. The Green Paper suggested that the credit might be paid to either mothers or fathers. This aspect of the proposal met with such violent opposition from family and women's organisations that the Government quickly agreed that the new credit should be paid to the mother. Once this commitment was given it was clear that the scheme entailed a double transference of income. The poorest families who were not claiming the full value of child tax allowances would receive a net increase of family income. For many other families, the main effect of the proposal was to transfer income from the husbands, who would lose their tax allowances, to wives, who would pick up the new payment at the post office.

The tax credit proposals were considered in detail by an all party Select Committee at the House of Commons. One key question to which the Committee addressed itself was the trade union reaction to what has since become known as the switch from the pocket to the purse. After discussing this aspect of the scheme with trade union leaders the committee was able to report 'We would stress that the General Council (of the TUC) are prepared to defend a decision to pay the child credits to the mother in spite of the implied loss to the father's pay packet.' While the Labour Party did not accept the tax credit proposals in their entirety, there was agreement across party lines about the development of a new child benefit, although each party christened the same reform with their own name.

Labour's response

Following the publication of the Select Committee report, *Labour's Programme 1973* — the major policy document Labour produced while it was in opposition — outlined a two-pronged attack on poverty. The first was to make the tax system more progressive and the second 'will be the new (child) benefit.' This commitment was written into the 1974 manifestoes. In its February Manifesto Labour pledged to 'help the low paid and other families in poverty by introducing a new system of child cash allowances for every child, including the first, payable to the mother'. In October the Party expressed a similar commitment and it was these promises which formed the basis of the Child Benefit Bill which was given a second reading in May 1975. In introducing the reform the Social Services

Secretary, Barbara Castle, commented, 'It is appropriate that this measure should be put before Parliment in International Woman's Year . . . It may be premature to talk of giving the wife and mother her own wage, but she certainly needs control of her own budget if the family is to be fed and clothed.' Sensing the importance of the switch from wallet to purse the Secretary of State went on to say 'It is right that I should pay a tribute to the trade union movement, which has always supported that formula (the switch from wallet to purse) although the unions frankly recognise this formula would affect their members' take home pay.'(12) Efforts were made to get written into the bill a starting date for the new benefit but these were rejected by the Government as being unnecessary.

A shoddy compromise

The first leaks on the cabinet debate on the child benefit scheme reached me in the Autumn of 1975 when ministers were discussing the starting date for the new scheme. The expectations of family and poverty groups were that the scheme would come into effect in April 1976. Papers presented to the cabinet vetoed this starting date on the grounds of cost, but ministers were advised to offer something in order to distract attention from the postponement. And as is so often the case, out of the vacillations of politicians was born a wretched little hybrid scheme which went under the title of CHIB — the child interim benefit.(13) This new benefit gave an extra £1.50 per week family allowance to the first children of single parent families. But not all first children of single parent families received the benefit; those drawing supplementary benefit or national insurance benefits were excluded. The papers presented to cabinet commended the scheme on the grounds of its cheapness. There was no underselling here. The full cost of the child interim benefit totalled £18 million a year.

I was given further information in April 1976 on the debate then taking place in Cabinet about the level at which the child benefit should be set when it was finally brought into operation in the April of the following year. On April 8 1976, three days after Mr Callaghan's appointment as Prime Minister, a reshuffled cabinet received a memorandum from the Secretary of State for Social Services, David Ennals, who had that day taken over from Barbara Castle. This memo spelt out that families with children were now getting substantially less support than the Tories provided in 1970, 1971 and 1972, and less than the Labour Government provided in the late 1960s. The Ennals' memo concluded with the words: 'If we continue to let child support be eroded by inflation, the whole scheme would be condemned as a trick to give children less, not more'.

Second thoughts

The debate amongst ministers staggered on throughout April. Cabinet minutes for April 29 recorded the Secretary of State as saying that failure to increase the real level of support for families would add to the difficulties in negotiating pay policy with TUC as well as hardening their resistance to a phasing out of food subsidies. It was at this Cabinet meeting that members began to discuss the effects of withdrawing child tax allowances on the negotiations for Stage III of incomes policy. The cabinet concluded that it might be best to postpone the child benefit if the funds were not available to pay an acceptable rate. Sensing the danger, David Ennals outlined the obstacles to a postponement at the following cabinet meeting. Some of the objections were administrative; for example, what was going to happen to the building and the staff who were now in post to administer the new scheme? He also argued that the Government would be accused of bad faith if it reneged on the scheme.

Despite this warning it was after this cabinet meeting that the Prime Minister began working behind the scenes. At a cabinet meeting a few days later he reported receiving an excellent report from the Whip's office which had created considerable doubts in his own mind about the political implications of introducing child benefit. After surveying opinion the new Chief Whip, Michael Cocks, reported to Cabinet that the introduction of child benefit in April 1977 would have grave political consequences which had not been foreseen when the bill went through the House of Commons. Cabinet members were led to believe that the Chief Whip's survey had been conducted on backbench opinion. It later emerged that the Chief Whip had only discussed this issue with members of the Whip's office.

In the ensuing discussion cabinet ministers expressed the belief that the distribution effects of child benefit between husband and wife could not be sold to the public before the scheme was brought in, a full twelve months later. However, the cabinet was aware that a scuttling of a major manifesto pledge would also have to be sold to the public, but it was believed that this task could be achieved within a matter of days.

Deception

As leaks on cabinet discussions had reached *The Times* throughout this period, I did not make use of the information I had received. The first public use of the cabinet papers I made was information provided to Hugh Herbert the *Guardian*'s social services correspondent, a few days after this cabinet debacle and a few days before the crucial meeting of the Labour Party/TUC Liaison Committee. The leak appeared to have some effect, for a statement issued by the liaison committee after its meeting declared 'It is of the utmost importance' that the scheme (referring to the issue of child poverty) should provide 'benefit generous enough to represent a determined and concerted attack on the problem'.

The full trade union delegation at that meeting did not know that a small group of union leaders — those who lead the trade union side on the National Economic Development Council — had arranged to see the Chancellor of the Exchequer and other senior ministers later in the day. At a cabinet meeting on the following day the Prime Minister asked the Chancellor to report on this meeting with TUC chiefs. The TUC had been asked to agree to a postponement of the child benefit scheme for three years because of the effect the loss of child tax allowances would have on take-home pay. The cabinet minutes record: 'On being informed of the reduction in take-home pay, which the child benefit scheme would involve, the TUC representatives had reacted immediately and violently against its implementation, irrespective of the level of benefit which would accompany the reduction in take home pay.'

A rather different picture emerges from the minutes of the TUC General Council following the meeting with the Chancellor. Trade union leaders had been told by the Chancellor that 'the majority view' of the Cabinet was in favour of deferring the scheme beyond 1977. The Cabinet, said Mr Healey, had taken the view that 'in present circumstances the effect of the removal of the tax allowances on take-home pay would be catastrophic'. The minutes record David Basnett as saying that there had been pressure from Labour MPs 'not to implement the full scheme for the simple reason that it meant a transfer from the wallet to the purse'. The complicity was complete when the Secretary of State announced a postponement of the scheme on the ground of trade union objections, which had been gained by informing TUC representatives of the supposed opposition to the scheme amongst Labour backbenchers. Once again family benefits had been presented in terms of a cut in wage packets rather than of increasing family income. The campaign against a living wage had now turned full circle.

The fiasco over child benefits raised some very important lessons on the way the cabinet makes and unmakes major decisions. It's quite clear from the cabinet minutes that no minister really understood the reasons for this major commitment. The effect on take home pay had *always* been the point. One could only wonder on how many other issues there is this kind of confusion and basic ignorance.

The post-mortem

The cabinet minutes also gave a clear idea of how the present cabinet views political activity and how a radical government can become managers rather than reformers. When the Prime Minister drew up the criteria to decide which of his cabinet colleagues would be questioned by Sir Douglas Allen — the head of the Home Civil Service who was appointed to inquire into the leak — the transformation from reformers to managers was complete. Cabinet ministers were interviewed if it was known that they were committed to the child benefit scheme (a pledge in Labour's 1974 manifestoes), or they believed in more open government (another pledge in both election manifestoes) or if they were deemed to be politically motivated (an attribute one might expect in all professional politicians of cabinet rank earning up to £20,000 a year). Cabinet members were to be interviewed if they qualified on one or more of these grounds, yet only a third of the cabinet were questioned. One cabinet minister was successful in resisting interrogation by Commander Habershon of the Special Branch, who followed up on Sir Douglas Allen's inquiry, by informing the Prime Minister that if he was ordered to meet Commander Habershon he would request Lord Hailsham to be present with him at the meeting. Commander Habershon did not bother this Secretary of State further.

The investigations by Sir Douglas Allen and the Special Branch failed to find the culprit. One reason for this was that since the first disclosure of cabinet discussions on the CHIB back in the Autumn of 1975 I had always referred to the source or sources by the code name Deep Throat. This had a number of advantages. In the first place it allowed me to talk freely about the leak without any fear of giving any clues in an unguarded moment. As importantly, it allowed me to talk publicly with Deep Throat while people were present without in any way raising suspicions. Once the official investigations were underway into the cabinet leak, it was of crucial importance that Deep Throat and I knew what each other was thinking and saying. I relayed as much information as possible about my moves, what I was and was not saying, over the radio and television and in the newspapers. I also asked Deep Throat's advice on what I should be doing. Whenever Deep Throat was part of a group of people who wanted to talk about the cabinet leak I would ask what they thought Deep Throat would suggest as the next move. Much advice was offered by this means, including the crucial advice from Deep Throat. By using this technique, and with the help of the media who relayed so much information as legitimate news, I never contemplated clandestine meetings, or trying to make contact by telephone. The tapping of my telephones were therefore unnecessary.

Alleged small textual inaccuracies in the *New Society* leak article also appeared to put the authorities off the scent. Because of these Sir Douglas Allen was led to conclude that the leak was based on information scribbled down in haste by a junior civil servant. And when the Prime Minister commented upon this very fact in the House of Commons I became aware of the extent to which errors creep into a dictated text. Moreover, once the *New Society* article had been dictated I destroyed all the papers. I then noticed that the dates of cabinet meetings in the typescript did not conform to the normal days on which the Cabinet meets — Tuesdays and Thursdays. I therefore altered a number of dates to correspond to the traditional pattern of meetings. Although this introduced further minor errors into the text, it also misled the bloodhounds.

Consequences

Deep Throat's bravery resulted in a number of public gains. The first tangible result from the leaks was the Prime Minister's statement to the House of Commons that he could no longer defend his strongly held opposition to reforming the Official Secrets Act. But, as with the commitment on child benefits, a vigilant campaign has been mounted and will continue to act as a watchdog over the Government's proposed reforms in this field. As events are beginning now to unfold it appears as though the Government is attempting to bring forward a limited reform which will result in any caught leakers being successfully prosecuted, while on the other hand maintaining the maximum secrecy on the activities of British governments.

But far and away the most important result of the leaks was the public outcry over the Government's proposed intentions which prevented them from scuttling, and scuttling, and scuttling again on their commitment to child benefits. April 1976 saw the beginnings of the child benefit scheme with cash payments being paid to mothers in respect of all their children, and not limited to second and subsequent children as it was under the Family Allowance Act. But does the new benefit restore the level of family support which operated in the late sixties or, as the Secretary of State pointed out to the Cabinet colleagues, to the level given by the Heath Government in the early 1970s?

A restatement

What child support there is is more equitably distributed today than in the late 1960s. This has not been brought about by the direct actions of government but by inflation. Successive governments have failed to raise the tax threshold — the point at which we begin to pay tax — in the line with rising prices. As a result the number of workers brought within the tax net has grown so that today practically everybody in full-time work pays income tax and almost all families now offset part of their tax liability against their child tax allowances. As we have seen, one of the major reasons for child benefits was that the earnings of poor families were too low for them to claim the full benefit of child tax allowances. Under the old system of family allowances and child tax allowances, successive chancellors had the means of directly changing the relative tax burden of families with children by increasing tax allowances. Since 1948 there have been nine changes on this front compared to only five changes in family allowances. But the old prejudice against family allowances appears to have been grafted onto the new child benefit. In the last two budgets Mr Healey made tax concessions equalling £3.5 billion. All that has been given to children, and that mainly as a result of the cabinet papers leak, has totalled a mere £330 million. Yet, in a statement before his last budget, Mr Healey ruled out the possibility of giving extra money in the form of child benefits as 'these would work against people without children'. In 1970 a Labour Government faced the charge that the poor had become relatively poorer under Labour. If this prejudice forms the basis of Mr Healey's main April budget, then this Government will face the charge this time that families, both rich and poor alike, have lost out under a Labour administration.(14)

The overwhelming majority of people would agree that families with children need a larger income than other households. But how much more, and does the present horizontal distribution of income reflect adequately family needs? I believe not. If we take two households, one earning £55 a week gross and the other £75 gross it is possible to see how our present system of taxation and benefits make allowances for children. Expressing the net income of a single person on £55 as a 100 per cent we find that a household with one child, in other words, with two additional mouths to feed, has an income of only 13 per cent more than a single person, after we take into account the effects of taxation and child benefits. At the other extreme, a household with four children, in other words with five more mouths to feed than a household of a single person, has a net income that is less than 35 per cent more than a single person's.

A similar picture emerges for those on average earnings. A one-child family's net income is only 10 per cent greater than a single person's, and a four-child family's income is less than 27 per cent greater than a single person's. These small differences in the net income of households responsible for children compared with childless households is a marked feature right up the income scale.

This position demands action in the next years Budget (1978). And the Government should use next April's fiscal changes for beginning a campaign to persuade people to take a life-cycle view of their earnings. The businessman and sociologist Seebohm Rowntree carried out a first study in York in 1899. As well as measuring the extent of poverty in a prosperous town at the turn of the century, Rowntree introduced us to the idea of the cycle of poverty. Specifically he wrote:

> The life of a labourer is marked by five alternating periods of want and comparative prosperity. During early life, unless his father is a skilled worker, he will probably be in poverty; this will last until he, or some of his brothers or sisters, begin to earn money and thus augment their father's wage sufficiently to raise the family above the poverty line. Then follows the period on which he is earning money and living under his parents' roof; for some portion of this period he will be earning more money than is required for lodging, food, and clothes. This is his chance to save money. If he has saved enough to pay for furnishing a cottage, this period of comparative prosperity may continue after marriage until he has two or three children, when poverty will again overtake him. This period of poverty will last for ten years, i.e. until the first child is 14 years old and begins to earn wages; but if there are more than 3 children it may last longer. While the children are earning, before they leave the home to marry, the man enjoys another period of prosperity — possibly, however,

only to sink back into poverty when his children have married and left him, and he himself is too old to work, for his income has never permitted his saving enough for him and his wife to live upon for more than a very short time'.(15)

It was this information on the life cycle of poverty which stirred Eleanor Rathbone in those early days of the campaign to relate family income to its needs. But the same picture of periods of relative prosperity and relative deprivation emerged from an examination of today's data. Looking at the life time's pay of a low-wage earner, Tony Atkinson has shown that these earnings 'are less than sufficient to meet the supplementary benefit plus 40 per cent standard in earlier years; they are also insufficient as a man nears retirement when his earnings drop and his wife's earnings cease'. Rowntree's life cycle of poverty still stands for many of today's families. 'Income is likely to fall short of needs when there are dependent children and in old age. The period of "comparative" plenty comes in the 40s and 50s, when there are no dependent children and both husband and wife are at work. Even in this period, however, the family's disposable income is only £5 above its needs, so that the margin is not particularly generous. At this point, the low pay of women becomes of considerable importance to the family'.(16)

The link between bearing the responsibility for children, or being old, and being in poverty can also be seen from an examination of those claiming supplementary benefits. Almost five million people are now regularly dependent on supplementary benefits raising their income to the state poverty line. Of this total only 15 per cent, or less than 1 in 7, are not pensioners or responsible for children. But even this percentage underestimates the link between periods of dependency and poverty, for some of those single claimants will themselves be claiming benefit in their own right, although members of a family dependent on supplementary benefits.

The development of a really generous system of child benefits, similar to that in operation in most EEC countries, is now urgent. It is urgent because it is the most effective way of combating family poverty. It is also urgent because it is the most effective way of relating family income to family needs. It is also urgent because it is the most effective way of levelling out a life time's earnings; that periods of childlessness are matched with slightly higher taxation so that when, as so often happens, a family takes on the responsibility for children and with it loses the wife's income, the family income will be increased substantially by child benefits.

11 Poverty, Growth and the Redistribution of Income

This essay was first presented as a paper to the proceedings of Section F (Economics) of the British Association for the Advancement of Science, 1978. It was first published in *Slow Growth in Britain*, edited by W. Beckerman (OUP, 1979). Like 'Limits to Redistribution', it has become more relevant since its publication. The basis of the post-war political consensus has been that programmes of reform are paid for from growth and not by redistribiution of existing resources. This essay shows that economic forces resulting in the massive rise of unemployment, together with the demographic changes giving rise to a significant increase in one parent families, call for a redistribution of existing resources in order to prevent cuts in the living standards of the poor. The Labour party has yet to fully respond to this challenge.

Introduction

A shared assumption among many politicians and most of the electorate is that normal times in Britain are characterised by full employment and steadily rising national income. Memories are short, and it is to the fifties and early 1960s that most people look in support of this view. But if we take a wider panoramic view of the century a rather different picture emerges. Viewed historically, the boom years following the Second World War are very much the exceptional period for Britain during this century. The title of this section of the Association's meeting suggests that this is now being recognised.

This paper explores three themes. The first section examines what is usually meant by the term poverty, how the numbers of poor have grown in the post-war boom years and the extent to which their rising living standards have been a consequence of the general living standards rather than of a redistribution of income. The second section argues that a relatively slow growth rate will increase the numbers of the poor and the ranks of those on low income will be swelled at the same time by demographic changes. Real incomes of the poor will therefore fall in the immediate future unless an increasing share of the GDP is allocated to them. The third section concludes on the note that a period of relatively slow growth will test the genuineness of the concern expressed by most shades of opinion about the poor in the post-war period. Will this concern be translated into action entailing a redistribution of income to maintain the present real income of the poor, let alone improve their relative position?

The post war record

The Supplementary Benefits Commission's scale rates (plus an addition to meet housing costs) provide a minimum income for those people who are unable to work. Since 1965 Parliament has made an annual review of the scale rates, but this minimum income for those outside the labour market is far from generous. For example, a mother is expected to cover all the needs of a child under ten on less than £1.03 a day (updated for 1980 figures). How many people in the years since 1948 have been living at this minimum level of income approved by Parliament?

The number of households dependent on supplementary benefit has risen from a little over a million in 1948 to almost three million by 1976. But these figures do not measure the total numbers of persons whose living standards are determined by supplementary benefit payments. If dependants are included with the numbers of claimants, the total rises to around five million. In addition there is a growing number of persons in households whose incomes are below the supplementary benefit level. The latest data are again for 1976. There were then 1,350,000 families containing 2,280,000 persons, living on incomes below the supplementary benefit level.

As well as showing a rise in the numbers dependent on supplementary benefits, the figures also illustrate how the face of poverty has changed over the past thirty years. In 1948, 63 per cent of supplementary benefit claimants were retirement pensioners. By 1976 this proportion had fallen to 57 per cent. If the numbers of persons dependent on supplementary benefit are considered, as opposed to those claimants drawing benefit, the decline in the percentage of old people living at the officially approved minimum level of income is more marked. In 1955 retirement pensioners and their dependants made up 61 per cent of persons dependent on national assistance payments. By 1976 this proportion has fallen to 42 per cent.

Some critics argue that the supplementary benefit levels should not be taken as a measurement of poverty over time. As living standards rise so too does Parliament increase the weekly payments made by the SBC. Politicians have not been slow to argue that an increase in the numbers of SB claimants is due to a more generous definition of poverty rather than an increase in the numbers of poor. For example, in the run-up to the 1970 General Election, the present Secretary of State for Social Services, David Ennals, was involved in a dispute about whether the poor had become relatively poorer during the period of the first two Wilson Governments. The Minister did not reply directly to this charge made by CPAG, but asserted that 'the supplementary benefit scale rates have been raised every year since the Government took office. They are now, in real terms, 18 per cent higher than the 1964 national assistance scale. One result has been to increase the numbers of people drawing benefit by 600,000.'(1)

What was not in dispute was that supplementary benefits had risen in real terms — comparing their value at the time of each uprating. But the Minister's argument that the numbers of poor had increased due to changes in the scale rates was only valid if their relative, as opposed to real, value had been increased. Did this in fact happen?

Weighing the evidence

The evidence is somewhat confusing. If the value of supplementary benefit payments is expressed as a percentage of gross and net earnings for each year since 1948 the following two trends are discernible. Looking over the whole period it is clear that the value of the scale rate as a percentage of gross earnings, while fluctuating, has changed very little. A different picture emerges if we consider the value of benefits against net earnings. Because the tax burden has increased for working households the supplementary benefit poverty line measured against net earnings has increased substantially over the period. A major change occurred in 1965 in the value of what is called the ordinary scale rate. A similar ratchet effect in the value of the long-term rate took place in 1974.

However, an important study published recently suggests that the relative value of benefits has remained fairly constant in the post-war period. The authors of the report were aware of the difference in the values of the supplementary benefit scale rates when measured against gross and net earnings but reworked the data on 'an equivalent net income basis'. Their results showed that 'the relative living standards of the poor appeared to remain approximately constant between 1953/4 and 1971, at about 49 per cent of the median for the 5th percentile and about 58 per cent for the 10th percentile'.(2) The study went on to say: 'This reflects the much sharper rise between 1953/4 and 1971 in the direct tax burden of median households (4.3 per cent of gross incomes of 14.8 per cent) than of poor households (1.8 per cent to 3.2 per cent). And the final observation was: 'It is perhaps best to conclude that the evidence points to neither a significant deterioration nor an improvement in the relative income of the poor over this period'.(3)

If the relative income of the poor has not improved, in other words, if there has not been a redistribution to those on low incomes, to what extent and by what means have the living standards of the poor changed in the post-war period?

This was also a question which concerned the poverty study just cited, that was carried out on behalf of the National Institute of Social and Economic Research. No one would dispute the fact that the living standards of the poor have risen during the post-war period. The extent of the increase can be seen from one of the NIESR's calculations. When the real value of national assistance for 1953/4 was held constant, throughout the post-war period and up until 1971, the numbers of poor dropped from a total of 2.4 millions to 300,000. Alternatively, by taking the real value of assistance in 1971, and applying it to households' incomes in 1953/4, the authors found a total of 10.6 millions poor in the earlier year.(4) On the basis of these calculations the study concluded that as 'the substantial rise of about 75 per cent recorded in the real income of the poor over the last two decades is not attributable to any appreciable change in their relative standards it must reflect participation in a general improvement of living standards'.(5)

The Royal Commission on the Distribution of Income and Wealth undertook a similar analysis which was reported in its lower income reference. It concluded that the rise in the living standards of the poor was due to the general rise in prosperity rather than a redistribution of resources. Taking 1961 as its bench mark, and measuring the period up to 1974/5, the Commission found that the average real income of the lowest three tenths of family units increased by roughly 40 per cent, in line with the growth of GNP of about 38 per cent.(6)

It also illustrated the importance of economic growth in raising the living standards of the poor. The Commission took 1961 as its base line and calculated the numbers in poverty in 1975 if the 1961 poverty line income was maintained in real terms only. Their finding was that the proportion of family units below the 1961 level in 1975 was reduced by over a half to about a tenth, observing 'This shows how the growth of the economy operated over this period to permit the level of income of those on the lowest quarter to be raised'.(7)

Slow growth and the numbers of poor

Research from the NIESR and the Royal Commission suggests that the increase in the living standards of the poor during the post-war period has not been due to a redistribution of resources. Rather, the rise in living standards of those on low incomes has occurred because they have shared in the country's increasing prosperity. A period of sustained slow growth could, therefore, result in a brake being applied to any improvements in the poor's living standards. There are four reasons, however, why a period of slow growth must be matched by a period of positive redistribution of resources towards those at the bottom of the income distribution.

The first concerns the actual standard of living on which a growing number of poor people are required to live. There is no dispute that the poor have shared in the increased prosperity of the last thirty years or so. But what has to be faced is whether the living standards of today's poor are at an unacceptably low level compared with the overall prosperity of the community in which they live. For example, a couple with two children on the ordinary scale rate receive a benefit valued at only 40 per cent of average earnings. Research cited earlier illustrate the need for an improvement in the relative incomes of those living around the supplementary benefit level, particularly if they have children.(8)

There is a second reason why a period of slow or nil growth should be accompanied by a policy of redistribution. Despite the growth in national income, low pay remains a serious problem and the dimension of this problem can be seen by looking at the relative rewards of lower paid workers as well as the numbers earning their poverty. Earnings data were first collected for male workers in 1886. Data on earnings were then collected spasmodically up until 1970. What is of importance to our considerations is whether the value of the earnings of the poorest workers has risen compared to median earnings during a period of more rapid growth and rising prosperity. The value of median earnings for manual men and women workers is given in Table 11.1.

The figures show a remarkable stability in relative earnings. In 1886

Table 11.1 Weekly earnings of manual workers, lowest decile as a percentage of median earnings, 1886–1977

Year	*Manual Men*	*Manual Women*
1886	68.6	—
1906	66.5	—
1938	67.7	64.3
1960	70.6	72.0
1963	70.7	68.5
1964	71.6	65.1
1965	69.7	66.5
1966	68.6	66.3
1967	69.8	66.1
1968	67.3	71.1
1970	67.3	69.0
1971	68.2	70.2
1972	67.6	68.9
1973	67.3	69.2
1974	68.6	69.1
1975	69.2	68.4
1976	70.2	67.8
1977	70.6	70.3

Source: Figures for 1886–1974 taken from *British Labour Statistics Yearbook*, 1974, Table 52, HMSO 1977. Figures from 1975 taken from *New Earnings Survey* 1977, Table 15, HMSO 1978.

the value of the lowest decile of manual men workers was 68.6 per cent of median earnings. By 1977 the value of the poorest 10 per cent of manual men workers had been edged up by two percentage points.

The first earnings data on manual women workers were collected in 1938 and the table shows a greater fluctuation in the earnings of the poorest women workers. For example, in 1938 the value of the lowest decile expressed as a percentage of the median earnings was 64.3 per cent while thirty years on this had risen to 71.1 per cent. Since then, however, the earnings of the poorest women workers show the same kind of stability as can be noticed in the data on their male counterparts. By 1977 the value of the lowest decile was 70.3 per cent of median earnings. The overall impression given by the data is therefore clear: the prosperity of the post-war years has done little to improve the relative rewards of those who earn their poverty be they male or female workers. If the relative earnings of the poorest in work have remained fairly stable what has happened to the numbers who are low paid?

There are three ways of categorising low-paid workers. They are defined by the National Board for Prices and Incomes as being in the lowest decile of the earnings distribution. While this approach has some advantages, its main disadvantage is that, with an unequal distribution of income, there will always be a lowest decile of male earners. It, therefore, holds no value for policy makers who wish to measure the success or otherwise of actions aimed against low pay. For this reason increasing emphasis is put on measuring the numbers of low paid as those who either earn less than their supplementary benefit entitlement, or who earn a wage packet which is less than a target figure of average earnings.

Data on the numbers earning less than their supplementary benefit entitlement have been published for each year since 1972. However, the data for the two earliest years are not comparable with the sequence from 1974 when the self-employed were included in the FES calculations for the first time. The numbers earning less than the supplementary benefit poverty line for each year since 1974 are given in Table 11.2. It is important to note, however, that the total of low-paid workers will include those who have been unemployed or sick for less than three months and whose household income, when they were in work, was less than the SB rate. But it is also necessary to stress that the data exclude many low paid workers with working wives whose additional income brings the household income above the statutory poverty line.

Table 11.2 Incomes below supplementary benefit level of those normally in full-time work or self-employed.

GREAT BRITAIN	*Thousands*	
Year	*Income below supplementary benefit*	
	Families	Persons
1974	130	360
1975	210	630
1976	290	890

Source: DHSS. (For more up-to-date data see page 69.)

While it must be amphasised that these FES data are open to a fairly wide margin of error, the trend from the table is nevertheless clear. The number of poverty wage earners has risen from 130,000 in 1974 to 290,000 two years later.

Measuring low pay overall

The numbers earning less than the supplementary benefit payments which would be made to them if they were not working is but the tip of the low pay iceberg. An overall measurement of the extent of low pay comes from looking at the TUC 1974 minimum wage target which was set at £30 a week or two-thirds of average male earnings. Although the TUC has been reluctant to revise this money target, the Government's latest white paper on inflation up-dates the target figure for 1977. Taking the two-thirds minimum wage target, we see from the 1977 New Earnings Survey that 1.1 million men and 2.7 million women workers, a total of 3.8 million adult workers overall, earn below two-thirds of average earnings, even after taking into account overtime. If the earnings data were analysed without overtime the numbers rise to 1.7 million to 2.8 million respectively, a total of 4.5 million adult workers.(9)

The rising prosperity of the fifties and early sixties failed to eradicate low pay, however low pay is defined. The recession following the OPEC price rises has resulted in a dramatic increase in the numbers who earn their poverty. The growing number of low paid alone makes a powerful case for redistribution. But there are additional reasons why a period of slow growth should be accompanied by an attack on low pay. Recently we have become aware of how low-pay is not only an immediate, but also an indirect cause of poverty. Tony Atkinson summed up the evidence on this point by observing

> that low earnings are more important than an analysis of the immediate causes of poverty would suggest. Low pay must be seen more generally as a disadvantage in the labour market, and as associated with high incidence of job instability and ill-health and with the absence of fringe benefits. The low-paid worker is more vulnerable to the interruption or loss of earning power, and lacks the resources to meet such needs. Low earnings mean that people cannot save for emergencies or for old age... In these and other ways low pay plays an important role in the cycle of poverty'.

To which he adds 'low pay is a thread which runs throughout people's working lives and beyond into retirement, and what may appear at first sight to be "bad luck" is likely to be related to labour market disadvantage. Poverty does not happen to just anyone'.(10)

The case for redistribtuion

But redistribution is demanded because a period of slow-growth will itself worsen further the low pay problem in the following ways. As Atkinson noted, those in low-paying occupations and industries tend to be more vulnerable to unemployment. In part this is due to the fact that the low paid are concentrated in older industries employing outdated technologies which are more vulnerable to economic fluctuations. It is also due to the fact that unemployment is selective in its effects, bearing more heavily on women, the unskilled, coloured workers and those at the beginning or end of their working lives — all those groups in fact who are most likely to be found amongst the ranks of the low paid. Although we have very little information on the association between unemployment and wage rates at an aggregate level, these factors inevitably tend to depress the bargaining strength of workers who are already poorly paid.

Earlier we saw that a large number of workers on low basic rates of pay lift themselves and their families out of poverty by working overtime. The latest estimates, for 1977, suggest that three-quarters of a million more people would have been low paid if they had not worked overtime. Indeed, the numbers of low-paid men increase by over 60 per cent if overtime is taken out of the calculations. This being the case, the cutbacks in overtime and shift working which inevitably accompany periods of slow or nil growth are likely to have a severe impact on the living standards of the low paid.

Moreover, we know that many families in which the breadwinner is low paid are forced to supplement these earnings through a second wage. Indeed, the Royal Commission on the Distribution of Income and Wealth cited evidence showing the proportion of working families in poverty would increase three-fold if married women did not go out to work. Since married women are known to be highly vulnerable to unemployment, the recession will again reduce the family living standards of the low paid.(11)

The third reason supporting the case for a period of sustained redistribution is that the years of slow economic growth will be marked by an increase in the numbers made poor by unemployment. At the time of writing, the numbers of registered unemployed stand at around 1.5 million. The latest estimates from the Department of Employment project a rise in the labour force both in the five years up to 1981 and in the following five years. The projected increase in the labour force during the first five year period is put at a little under half a million (488,000). The projected increase over the whole period up to 1986 is put at a little over one million (1,047,000).(12)

Unemployment and poverty

On the assumption that the current job market is unaffected by technological changes such as the rapid introduction of microprocessing, what growth rate is required to create new jobs to match the projected increase in the labour force, let alone reduce the current record post-war level of unemployment? The estimates vary from 3 per cent, from the Treasury, to a 4 per cent growth rate from Terry Ward and the Department of Applied Economics at Cambridge. Against these figures we have to put the current growth rate of the economy, of around 2 per cent, which is unlikely to be maintained next year. It is on the basis of a growth rate substantially below the level required to match the expected increase in labour supply that practically all forecasting organisations project a rise in the numbers of unemployed. For example, the Cambridge Group has estimated that the level of unemployment will be 2.25 millions in 1982, rising still further to 3.6 millions five years later. Unless there is a major programme of work sharing, or of early retirement, or of raising the age threshold to the labour market or of job creation, a period characterised by relatively slow growth rate will add to the numbers of unemployed. How will this affect the numbers of poor?

Unemployment causes poverty because it reduces the majority of workless to a low level of income. Loss of work is not countered adequately by national insurance payments. In *Social Insurance and Allied Services* Beveridge spelt out the two key principles of his social insurance scheme. One was that 'all the principal cash payments — for unemployment, disability and retirement will continue so long as need lasts'.(13) The Report laid down that to draw benefit the unemployed would be required to register for work and could be suspended from benefit if they left their previous employment without good cause or had similarly refused a job offered to them by the labour exchange. In addition Beveridge stipulated that the payment of benefit could be made conditional on the claimant's attendance at a training centre. Once these conditions were fulfilled (and they operate in today's scheme) Beveridge saw no objection to paying unemployment benefit for as long as unemployment lasted. Yet this aspect of the Beveridge scheme was not accepted. Up until 1966 a standard provision of seven months' unemployment benefit was made, on top of which further days could be added depending upon the claimant's insurance record. The maximum period during which benefit was paid during any one time amounted to 19 months. The introduction in 1966 of an earnings related benefit for the first six months of unemployment was accompanied by a reduction in the duration of flat-rate benefit for up to 12 months.

The second basic principle of the Beveridge scheme was the payment of insurance benefits at a level which put the claimant's income above the official poverty line. The Attlee Government brought the Beveridge scheme into operation in 1948 but insurance benefits were paid at a lower level than was originally envisaged. For example, in that year unemployment benefit was only 10p greater for a single person than the national assistance scale rate. As claimants on the latter benefit would also have their rent paid, beneficiaries with no other resources than their national insurance benefits would usually be eligible for national assistance as well. So despite the existence of the flat rate and earnings related unemployment benefit, increasing numbers of the unemployed during the post-war period are being pushed into poverty.

The post-war period has been characterised by two trends. The percentage of unemployed dependent exclusively on national insurance benefits has fallen for most years, irrespective of the level of economic activity. In 1948, 71 per cent of the workless were dependent only on unemployment pay. By last year this percentage had dropped to 33 per cent and this total includes those drawing the earnings related supplement. At the same time the numbers of unemployed who were dependent exclusively on supplementary benefit rose from 10 per cent in 1948 to 42 per cent last year. The numbers made poor by unemployment will continue to grow as the total army of jobless increases, unless major changes are made to the national insurance provisions for the unemployed. In a period of slow or nil growth these changes will need to be financed by redistribution of income.

Demographic causes of poverty

Besides the likelihood of the growth in unemployment, demographic changes are taking place which will also increase the number of households living on low incomes. One major change over the recent past which has affected the numbers of poor has been an increase in the numbers of elderly. However, projections over the next decade show the numbers of pensioners rising only moderately and that changes on this front are now unlikely to add significantly to the numbers on low incomes.(14)

A totally different picture emerges if we look at the likely increase in the numbers of one-parent families. Recently single-parent families have been increasing at a little over 6 per cent a year. If this rate of increase is maintained over the next decade the number of single-parent families will grow from a total of 798,000 in 1977 to 1,390,000 by 1987. The corresponding increase in the number of children cared for in these families will rise from 1,436,000 to 2,503,000 over the same period of time. How will these projections affect the numbers of poor?

At the present time 60 per cent of one-parent families are dependent on supplementary benefit. If the same ratio is maintained over the next decade we find the following numbers of single-parent families drawing benefit.

Table 11.3 Projected number of one-parent families on supplementary benefit

Year	*Numbers of families*	*Numbers of children*
1977	343,938	619,000
1982	453,998	817,000
1987	599,277	1,078,700

By 1982 we estimate that 454,000 single parent families will be drawing supplementary benefit, a total rising to 599,000 five years later.

There is therefore yet a further reason why a period of slow or nil growth will need to be accompanied by a redistribution in favour of the poor. All the projections cited above have been employed so that an estimate can be made of the likely repercussions on the social security budget. These projected social security costs, in 1977 prices, taking account of demographic changes among pensioners and one-parent families, together with the cost of paying benefit to a growing army of unemployed, are presented in table 11.4.

Table 11.4 Projected social security costs (in 1977 prices)

Year	*Unemployed £m*	*Pensioners £m*	*One parent families £m*	*Total £m*
1977	2090.3	7,109	537	9,736.3
1982	3258.9	7,348	709	11,315.9
1987	5214.3	7,391	936	13,541.3

From this we can see that if the real value of benefits paid to these three groups of beneficiaries is to be maintained, the social security budget will need to rise from a current level of £9.7 billion for the three groups to just over £13.5 billion by 1987.

What will happen to the living standards of the poor during a decade characterised by a slow or nil growth rate? At the present time 10.8 per cent of GNP is spent on social security. If the real living standards of beneficiaries are to be maintained without a policy of redistribution GNP will need to grow by 16.3 per cent (or at 3.3 per cent at year in the years from 1977 up to 1982,) and by 39.1 per cent (or at an annual rate of 3.9 per cent) in the years up to 1987. Few people predict a sustained rate of growth anywhere approaching these levels. A failure to achieve these rates will therefore mean a real cut in the living standards of the poor unless the coming decade is marked by a determined policy of redistributing resources.

Conclusion

The post-war boom years may well prove to be an exceptional period for Britain during this century. They have, nevertheless, been a period characterised by an all-party agreement on poverty with both the Conservatives and the Left supporting the view that improvements in the living standards of the poor should be one of the first calls on an ever expanding national product. The Left have gone further, and argued that greater equality can and should be brought about by staking a disproportionate claim on the fruits of growth for those on low income. This central pillar underlying much of the ideological consensus of the post-war years is now threatened by a period of slow or even nil growth. For there has been no political commitment to improving the living standards of the poor by means of a *redistribution* of income.

This paper has tried to show that the years of affluence have failed the poor in two very important respects. In the first place it has afforded them an unacceptably low relative standard of living. Moreover, it has done little to improve the relative earnings of the poverty wage-earner and has left an economy characterised by low pay.

On these grounds alone there is a powerful case for the next decade to be characterised by a policy of redistribution to the poor. But a period of slower nil growth will itself add to the pressures for redistribution, and thereby stand on its head the current political consensus about growth and rising living standards of the poor. A period of slow growth will see an increase in the numbers made poor by unemployment as well as an increase in the numbers on low income as a result of demographic changes. In a period of slow or nil growth the living standards of what will become an increasing army of poor people will therefore be reduced unless the increase is matched by a policy of redistribution, for this rise in the numbers of poor will require a real increase in the social security budget.

Finally, what do we mean when we talk about redistribution? While there is a strong moral case for redistributing along traditional lines — from rich to poor — such a policy alone will be inadequate to meet the challenge of maintaining, let alone increasing, the relative living standards of those on low incomes. Redistribution must also be pursued horizontally, from the childless to those with children. It will also need to take place from younger to older sections of the community, and from the consumers to some low-paid producers. And, in a period of rising unemployment, there will need to be a redistribution from those in work to the workless.

This plea will be met by the standard refrain that redistribution has already reached its limits. A period of slow growth will need to be accompanied by a much more critical look at the extent to which redistribution has occurred during the post-war years.(15) The 'reaching the limits of redistribution cry' has allowed the wealthy to become the convenient beneficiaries of their own propaganda — acting as a powerful sedative on the conscience of the privileged in our society. A period of slow economic growth is to be welcomed if it results in a realisation that at any time, and particularly when national income fails to grow, the crucial political question revolves around what can be justified as a fair distribution of existing income.

12 Limits to Redistribution: What Limits and What Kind of Redistribution?

This paper was first presented to the Coulston Symposium in 1979, and first published in Coulston Paper 31, *Income Distribution: the Limits to Redistribution* (Scientechnica, 1980). The paper questions the conventional wisdom that the post-war period has witnessed a significant redistribution of income from rich to poor. The changing burden of taxation, and the changing share in total revenue raised by different groups of the population, presents a very different picture to the conventional one of high tax-rates penalising the rich. A no-growth economy accompanied by a significant increase in the numbers of poor will call for not only a redistribution of existing resources from rich to poor, but also a redistribution from men to women, a redistribution over a person's lifetime so that the earnings of up to forty years are spread more equally over a lifetime of eighty or more years, as well as a redistribution from the state to the individual. I have explored these themes further in *Inequality in Britain: Freedom Welfare and the State*, Fontana, 1981.

The author acknowledges the help of Louise Burghes who prepared some of the material for the paper, and Chris Pond for checking the calculations.

Introduction

The debate on 'the limits to redistribution' is likely to be changed fundamentally by the Yom Kippur war. The slowing down of the world economy is beginning to have major political repercussions, not least on the question for distribution of income. The entering into what is generally agreed will be a period of slow economic growth brings to an end a chapter in post-war British politics. Until the 1973 oil crisis most discussion centred on redistributing newly created wealth. The first section of this paper looks at those forces which are beginning to emphasise the importance of redistributing existing wealth towards the poor.

This changing debate will need to be accompanied by widespread understanding of the current distribution of personal incomes. Since the Second World War, and, particularly, during the last ten years or so, there has been a powerfully orchestrated campaign asserting that the limits to redistribution have been reached. The second section of this paper critically looks at those assertions to show that while changes have occurred, the gains for those at the bottom end of the distribution have been very modest.

Living standards are not only affected by vertical changes in the distribution of incomes. The horizontal distribution is of equal importance, although it has hardly featured in the current debate. The final section of this paper looks at the extent to which households with children — whatever their level of income — have been losing out over the past twenty years or so, and questions those who assert that welfare provisions have adequately compensated for this trend.

The end of post-war consensus

Central to the post-war political consensus has been a set of beliefs stemming from the role performed by economic growth. The agent for lowering the political temperature, while at the same time removing the stains left by society's grosser forms of poverty, was a steadily rising national income.

As on so many issues, the clearest exponent of how to achieve simultaneously these two apparently contradictory goals was Anthony Crosland. Crosland believed growth provided the formula for leaving the rich rich, while also lessening the poverty of the poor. Writing after the 1970 election defeat, Crosland began with a frank admission; he'd been wrong on the question of growth: 'I was too complacent about growth in the *Future of Socialism*'. (1) He continued by listing the objectives to which Labour was still committed: the abolition of poverty, massive increases in public spending on education, housing and health, as well as mounting a major attack on environmental pollution. He continued his argument by adding, 'Certainly we cannot even approach our basic objectives with the present state of growth. For these objectives... require a redistribution of resources; and we shall not get this unless our total resources are growing rapidly.'

By developing this theme Crosland expressed one of the key premises of post-war consensus politics (italics added).

> I do not of course mean that rapid growth will automatically produce a transfer of resources of the kind we want; whether it does or not will

> depend on the social and political values of the country concerned. But *I do assert dogmatically that in a democracy low or zero growth wholly excludes the possibility*. For any substantial transfer then involves not only a relative but an absolute decline in real incomes of the better off half of the population . . . and this they will frustrate.

Crosland concluded by saying that in a utopia, or a dictatorship, it might be possible to transfer resources of a near or static GNP to the have nots, but 'In the rough democratic world in which we live, we cannot.'

New world

Slowly people are becoming aware that the current recession is different from previous swings in economic activity. Not only is unemployment higher than at any time during the past thirty-five years but neither government nor opposition holds out the prospect of returning to full employment in the near future. And while people puzzle over the economic indicators, little or no time is given to plotting the political consequences to our society of the loss of an ever rising national income.

One reason why we are so unprepared is that the scenarios presented by the revisionists exluded consideration of the world in which we now find ourselves. Crosland's argument is nothing if not comforting. Radicalism could be put on ice while awaiting a return to a high level of economic activity. The one possibility which was not discussed by Crosland, or subsequently by any of his disciples, was that a period of slow growth could result in real cuts in the living standards of the poor. But this is the future we may now face.

Powerful forces are at work increasing the numbers of poor. Slow growth will increase the numbers made poor by unemployment, and demographic changes are adding daily to the welfare roles. Real cuts in the poor's standard of living may therefore occur if the current period of slow growth is not accompanied by a redistribution of existing income to the poor.(2)

Unemployment

The first challenge to those arguing that the limits of redistribution have already been passed is being mounted from the dole queues. Today the unemployed number almost 1.5 million and the latest estimate from the Department of Employment projects a rise in the labour force of about half a million by 1982. On the assumption that the current job market is unaffected by technological change, it is estimated that a growth rate of between 3 and 4 per cent per annum is required to match the projected increase in the labour force, let alone reduce the current record post-war level of unemployment.

It is on the basis of a growth rate below the level required to match the expected increase in labour supply that practically all forecasting organisations project a rise in the numbers of unemployed. The Cambridge Group has estimated, for example, the level of unemployment at 2.25 millions in 1982. How will this growth in the ranks of the unemployed affect the social security budget?

Increasing unemployment will affect the amount spent on the social security budget in two ways. In the first place more claims will be made on the insurance benefits scheme as a greater number of people draw unemployment benefit. Many of the projected 2.25 millions will be eligible for national insurance benefits. Secondly, larger numbers of the unemployed will also be drawing supplementary benefit. If the Cambridge Group predictions are right, and the proportion of the unemployed drawing supplementary benefits remains the same as at present (which is unlikely because the proportion is increasing as the recession worsens), then by 1982 the numbers made poor by unemployment will have risen to over a million.

Demographic changes

At a time when the numbers of unemployed are likely to increase, demographic changes are taking place which will also increase the number of households on low income. The major change on this front is the increase in the numbers of single-parent families. Recently one-parent families have been increasing at a little over 6 per cent a year. If this rate of increase is maintained over the next five years one-parent families will grow from a total of 798,000 in 1977 to 1,053,400 in 1982. The corresponding increase in the numbers of children cared for in these families will rise from 1,436,000 to 1,896,000 over the same period of time. This increase in the number of one-parent families will have a major effect on the social security budget. At the present time 60 per cent of one-parent families depend on supplementary benefit. If the same ratio is maintained we can estimate that by 1982 there will be 454,000 single-parent families drawing supplementary benefit.

In making estimates about the future size of the social security budget, another group that must be taken into account are retirement pensioners. Although the number of retirement pensioners will not increase greatly in the next five or ten years (their numbers will in fact have declined by the turn of the century) expenditure on retirement pensions and supplementary pensions now accounts for over 50 per cent of the total social security budget.

It would be possible to continue these projections across the whole field of welfare state provisions. However, the full range of calculations have been excluded, partly because it is more difficult to estimate their likely financial consequences, but also because an analysis limited to those three groups of claimants — the unemployed, one-parent families and pensioners — clearly illustrates the challenge to the 'limits to redistribution' thesis which will be brought about by an increasing number of the poor if national income fails to grow at above the average post-war rate.

If the living standards of the poor are to be maintained at a time when the number made poor by unemployment, as well as the numbers of one-parent families in poverty, are growing, the social security budget will need to rise from the current level of £13.2 billion to £14.5 billion by 1982. At the present time 10.8 per cent of GNP is spent on social security payments. In considering the effects of increases amongst the unemployed and one-parent families only, we see that if the living standards of all beneficiaries are to be maintained without a policy of redistribution, GNP will need to grow by 9.7 per cent in the years up to 1982. Failure to achieve this rate of increase will not just mean, as Crosland predicted, a freezing of radical intent, but a cut in the living standards of the poor. It is this prospect which gives a renewed urgency to the issue of redistribution and belies those sweeping generalisations that claim we have already reached the limits to redistributing from the rich to the poor.

Vertical distribution of income

The most popularly presented view about changes in the distribution of income in this country is of an inexorable move towards greater equality. To what extent have variations between incomes diminished in the recent past; have these changes affected all or only part of the distribution; and what role has the direct tax system played in this process? These are the questions to which we now turn.

The two main sources of data on the distribution of personal incomes are The Survey of Personal Incomes and the Blue Book tables. The Survey of Personal Incomes was carried out in the tax year 1949/50, two studies were completed during the next ten-year period, and a study has been carried out every year since 1962. The

Blue Book tables begin in 1938 and were published for each year from 1949 except for a gap from 1967 to 1972/3. One of the useful tasks completed by the Royal Commission on the Distribution of Income and Wealth (referred to hereafter as the Royal Commission) was to fill this gap, and so complete data for recent years now exist for both series. What pattern of income distribution do they show?

First, a word of warning about the data. In the initial report on its standing reference, the Royal Commission summarised what are generally agreed to be the reasons why the Survey of Personal Incomes presents an inaccurate picture of total personal incomes.(3) Here it is necessary to emphasise the main reservations which stem from the fact that the data are derived from tax returns. As all income is not subject to tax, the survey based on tax returns cannot give a complete picture of the distribution. And even where the definition of income is more in line with a 'command over resources' approach, the Revenue doubt whether returns about fringe benefits are reported with complete accuracy.

A second disadvantage of using tax returns to construct data on income distribution is that, by definition, those below the tax threshold are excluded. As we will see later, the tax threshold has changed dramatically during the post-war period. The Royal Commission observed that the exclusion of those with incomes below the tax limits has considerable implications for the conclusions which can be drawn from the data, particularly when making comparisons during the pre- and post-war periods, when the number of taxpayers doubled. A third main distorting factor is that the Revenue is uncertain about the scale of tax evasion. Changes in the extent of evasion will place further limits on the use to which the data can be put in making comparisons over time.

The Blue Book tables are based on The Survey of Personal Income (SPI) tables of the distribution of total net income, supplemented by data from other sources, notably the DHSS and the Family Expenditure Survey (FES). Commenting on the Blue Book data the Royal Commission listed the advantages of using this source of information. They were the 'only official statistics compiled solely for the purpose of presenting information about the distribution of personal income' and 'we regard these CSO tables as the most valuable income statistics available'. But the Commission added an important rider: 'they retain many of the defects of the SPI data'.(4)

Official surveys

Bearing in mind how incomplete any snapshot is of the personal distribution of income from official data, let alone the hazards of presenting changes over time, what can be said about the changes in the personal distribution of income charted by these official sources of data? Is the popularly held view about the diminishing differences in personal incomes supported from these data? Of particular importance are the more recent changes since it was from the election of the Labour Government in 1964 that the most recent debate about high levels of taxation and the growing equality of income was initiated.

In one sense the pre-tax data support the view of a move towards greater equality in income. The Survey of Personal Incomes shows that since 1964 the share of pre-tax personal incomes going to the richest one per cent fell from 7.7 per cent to 5.9 per cent. A reduction in pre-tax income is also recorded for the following top four per cent in the income distribution, but the change is much smaller. If the richest 2–20 per cent are taken as a group we find that their share of pre-tax income remains almost unchanged throughout the period since 1964. Not surprisingly, therefore, the data show that the share going to the poorest 30 per cent remains fairly constant throughout the eleven years following 1964.

A similar picture emerges from the data on the post-tax distribution of income. Again there is a marked reduction in the share going to the top one per cent but the richest 2–10 per cent in the income distribution commanded almost the same share (17.9 per cent) in 1974/5 of total personal incomes as they did back in 1964 (18 per cent). Again the share of total personal incomes going to the poorest 30 per cent remains almost the same throughout the period since 1964, although it is important to bear in mind the qualifications cited earlier about changes in the tax threshold affecting the data on low-income earners.

To what extent does a different picture emerge from the Blue Book statistics? The years since 1964 record a similar reduction in the share of pre-tax income going to the richest one per cent. But, as with the Survey of Personal Incomes, the share of personal incomes commanded by the richest 2–10 per cent in the income distribition remains almost the same. During the same time, the poorest 30 per cent share rose from 9.5 per cent in 1964 to 10.8 per cent in 1974/5.

The post-tax data from the Blue Book shows a reduction in the share of total personal incomes commanded by the richest one per cent during the years since 1964, with their share falling from 5.3 per cent after tax to 4 per cent in 1974/5. But the share of the following nine per cent in the income distribution again shows a much smaller reduction of 0.6 percentage points. The poorest 30 per cent in the income distribution again record a small increase, with their share rising from 11.6 per cent in 1964 to 12.8 per cent eleven years later.

The official data do not therefore support the broad generalisation about the extent to which personal incomes have been redistributed from rich to poor in the post-war period, particularly over the years since 1964. Both series of data show a reduction in the share of the richest one per cent but with the richest 2–10 per cent of the population maintaining their share of personal incomes. The redistribution has been from the super rich to the very rich and the total personal income going to the poorest 30 per cent show an increase significantly smaller than the reduction witnessed by the richest one per cent of the population.

While this conclusion does little to support the view that we have reached the limits to redistribution with respect to levelling down top incomes, it leaves unexplained why most people regard the British tax system as a powerful engine grinding ever relentlessly towards a greater equality in personal incomes. To understand the basis of this misconception requires some discussion on what has been called the welfare state for the rich — or the growth of the tax allowance system.

Tax changes

One of the key changes in the British system of direct taxation occurred in 1920. Up until then the income of the poor was protected from taxation by the operation of an exemption system. Tax allowances could be claimed up to a certain level of income, but beyond this point all income became liable to tax. The budget of 1920 changed the British tax system at a stroke; from the exemption to an allowance system.(5) In that year taxpayers were allowed to set the tax allowance against their income no matter how large.

One major effect of changing from the exemption to an allowance system has been to decrease the size of the tax base. The most comprehensive study so far on the effects of tax allowances on the size of personal income subject to tax has been compiled by researchers at the Centre of Fiscal Studies at Bath University. In their book *Tax Expenditures in the UK*, Messrs Willis and Hardwick show that, largely because of tax allowances, 'only 45 per cent of total gross income is taxed at the present time.'(6) They also make a distinction between structural allowances, which are the main personal allowances, and non-structural allowances, such as mortgage interest relief. In the year 1973/4 Willis and Hardwick calculate that non-structural tax relief accounted for 15 per cent of gross personal income. Had this sum been taxed at the then standard rate, total income tax revenue would have increased by 32 per cent, allowing a reduction in the standard rate of 7p in the £.(7)

Growth in the tax allowance welfare state has reduced significantly the amount of personal income subjected to tax. But because the post-war period has been characterised by increasing public expenditure it has been necessary to widen the tax base by increasing the proportion of the workforce required to pay tax. This process has continued to such an extent that tax is now levied on those levels of income which are below the supplementary benefit poverty line and the eligibility threshold level for the family income supplement.

Governments have also tried to compensate for the loss of revenue entailed in granting tax allowances by subjecting that income which is liable to tax to high marginal rates. It is these higher marginal rates which make most of the running in the current debate on the supposed redistributional impact of direct taxation. But high marginal rates of taxation are necessary partly because of the loss of revenue from tax allowances, which have themselves resulted in a reduction in the total of personal incomes subjected to tax.

A few examples show the difference between the marginal and average rates for taxpayers on different levels of income. A single person on £1,000 a year faces a marginal tax rate of 25 per cent on each £1 increase in earnings, but has an average tax rate of 6.9 per cent. Likewise, while a single person on £20,000 a year faces a marginal tax rate of 75 per cent, this same tax payer's average tax rate is below 50 per cent. But while it is the average tax rate which is the more important in determining net income, it is the marginal rates which are quoted in public debate to support the unacceptable face of taxation thesis.

Both marginal and average rates of tax are further reduced below the nominal rates shown in Table 12.1 by the claiming of non-personal tax allowances, and as we can see from the data, these tax allowances are of greater cash and percentage value to higher income groups. The average deduction in the tax year 1974/5 for the richest one per cent of taxpayers amounted to £648. In stark contrast the average deduction in the sixth decile amounted to £34.

Group taxation

The emphasis given to the high marginal rates of tax has been important in creating the image that the increasing burden of tax has been borne by higher income groups. In considering for which income groups the limits of redistribution have been reached it is

Table 12.1 The value of deductions for mortgage and other allowable interest payments and charges and retirement annuity premiums, 1975

United Kingdom		*Income unit: tax unit*
Quantile group	*Deductions as a proportion of average income*	*Average value of allowance £p*
	%	
Top 1%	4.6	648
2–5%	4.7	286
6–10%	4.2	187
Top 10%	4.5	274
11–20%	3.8	138
21–30%	3.5	105
31–40%	3.2	81
41–50%	2.9	62
51–60%	2.0	34
61–70%	1.7	22
71–80%	1.0	10
81–90%	0.8	7
91–100%	2.0	12

Source: Derived from Tables E4, E5 and E6, Appendix E Reworked data from Royal Commission 1977, table 9.

Table 12.2 Income tax as percentage of income: percentage change between 1964/5 and 1977/8

Income in relation to average earnings	*Single person*	*Married couple*	*Married couple and two children*
	%	%	%
2/3 Av. Earnings	88	177	235(1)
Av. Earnings	47	72	306
2×Av. Earnings	33	49	122
5×Av. Earnings	42	40	51
10×Av. Earnings	31	32	33
20×Av. Earnings	15	14	15

Source: Reworked from TGWU (1976), updated.
(1) From 1970/71, no tax paid – 1964/65.

important to look at changes in the incidence of taxation, not only between individual taxpayers on different levels of income, but also at changes between different income groups. The changing incidence on individual taxpayers is presented in Table 12.2

A single person taxpayer on two-thirds average earnings at the beginning and end of the period under study faced an increased tax bill of over 88 per cent. The single person remaining on five times average earnings over the same period of time also faced an increase in the percentage of income paid in tax but it was only half that of the low wage earner on two-thirds average earnings. Similar increases occurred for workers on ten and twenty times average earnings for the periods 1964/5 to 1977/8 but their increases amounted to a little over 31 per cent and less than 15 per cent respectively.

Some groups might argue that the very highest income earners experienced smaller percentage increases in the incidence of taxation because they are already paying too high a percentage of their income in tax in the first place. This argument is weakened when an examination is made of the changing incidence of taxation on different income groups. The data in Table 12.3 give the changes in the percentage of total revenue raised from each decile group over the past 20 years.

When considering changes in the total revenue contributed by different decile groups over a period of time it is also necessary to bear in mind changes in the share of pre-tax income going to each of these groups. It is possible for the richest ten per cent to be contributing less of total revenue now than they did in 1959/60 because they now command a smaller percentage of total pre-tax personal income.

The Blue Book data show the share of personal incomes going to the top ten per cent in the income distribution fell by 9.5 percentage points during the period from 1959 to 1974/5. Part of the reason therefore why the richest ten per cent pay a smaller total share of all revenue raised now than twenty years ago is that their share of total pre-tax income has fallen. But as the Blue Book data makes clear, the change in pre-tax income is only one reason for the changing incidence in taxation between income groups. During the twenty-year period covered by the table the percentage of total tax paid by the top decile fell from 57 to 37 per cent, a fall much greater than the fall in pre-tax income. One important reason therefore why the richest ten per cent are contributing less to total revenue now is that over these years the tax system has become less progressive.

Data presented in this section do not support the thesis that we

Table 12.3 Percentage shares of tax paid by different income groups 1959/60(2) to 1974/5

Year(1)	*Top 10%*	*10–20%*	*20–30%*	*30–40%*	*40–50%*	*50–60%*	*60–70%*	*70–80%*	*80–90%*	*Bottom 10%*	*Total Tax (£m)*
1949/50	72	9	5	3	3	3	2	1	1	1	1,101
1959/60	57	12	7	6	5	4	4	3	1	1	1,735
1970/71	41	15	11	9	7	6	5	3	2	1	6,158
1971/72	39	15	12	9	8	6	5	3	2	1	6,356
1972/73	40	14	11	9	8	6	5	4	2	1	6,572
1973/74	38	14	12	9	8	7	5	4	2	1	8,045
1974/75	37	15	11	10	8	7	5	4	2	1	11,846
1975/76	35	15	12	10	8	7	5	4	3	1	15,987
1976/77(3)	34	14	12	10	8	7	6	5	3	1	18,300

Source: House of Lords *Hansard*, col. 739–40 January 31, 1978.

Notes: (1) Years up to and including 1972/3 take income tax and surtax together. Subsequent years relate to income tax (including higher rates and the additional rate on investment income).

(2) Married couples are counted as one taxpayer. Only tax paid by individuals (i.e. excluding trusts etc.) is included.

(3) 1976/77 is a provisional estimate.

have reached the limits of redistributing from those at the upper end of the distribution. The Survey of Personal Incomes and the Blue Book data show that while the share of pre- and post-tax income going to the very richest one per cent has shown a marked reduction, this reduction is less marked amongst the richest 10 per cent, and most of the redistribution which has taken place has been amongst the top 20 or 30 per cent of the distribution. The share going to the poorest 30 per cent of the population shows very little change over the last fifteen years. Indeed, far from reaching the limits of redistribution from the rich, the data on the incidence of taxation suggest that their burden has lessened somewhat in the recent past. For example, the share of total tax revenue contributed by the richest 10 per cent has fallen by a significantly greater extent than has their share of the total pre-tax income. Not surprisingly, therefore, the burden has increased for those lower down the distribution. But this has only been one change in the incidence of taxation. We now turn to examine the second fundamental shift in the incidence of taxation which has occurred in the post-war period.

Horizontal redistribution of income

Vertical changes in the distribution of the tax load are only part of the total change in the incidence of taxation through the past 20 years. At the same time there has occurred a major change in the horizontal incidence of taxation: from the childless onto those households responsible for children. This second trend can be illustrated in a number of ways.

For each household group, whether it is a single person or married couple or family with children, taxpayers are now required to begin to pay income tax at a lower level of average earnings. While more poorer people are now paying tax than in the immediate post-war period, households with children have been singled out for particularly harsh treatment. The tax threshold for a single person or married couple without children has fallen as a proportion of average earnings by 40.1 and 41.1 per cent. In contrast a fall of 56.9 and 58.5 per cent is recorded in the tax threshold for a married couple with three and four children.

We gain a clearer picture of changes in the tax burden for different households by looking at the percentage of income paid in tax and national insurance for households who are childless and those who are responsible for children. Information on this question for selected years since 1960 is set out in Table 12.4.

Table 12.4 Tax and national insurance contributions as a percentage of average earnings, plus family allowance/child benefit where appropriate

Year	*Single person*	*Married couple*	*Married couple with 2 children aged under 11*	*Married couple with 4 children aged under 11*
	%	%	%	%
1960–61	19.0	14.0	6.8	3.2
1964–65	23.4	18.4	9.7	5.1
1973–74	28.2	25.8	21.6	18.6
1977–78	32.2	28.1	24.4	21.1
1978–79	31.3	27.4	24.6	22.0

Source: Hansard, Vol 950, col 735–8, 25 May, 1978.

Again the two trends in the changing incidence of taxation are illustrated. The tax burden has increased for all groups but it has increased fastest for those households with children. A single person and married couple on average earnings in 1960/61 who were earning the same income during the current financial year experienced a 65 and 96 per cent increase in their tax bills. On the other hand, for a married couple with two and four children who also remained on average earnings, the tax burden rose by 262 and 588 per cent.

It would be wrong to assume that these changes have occurred evenly for all groups during the post-war period. The most recent period since 1974 illustrates how short-term gains can be chalked up for some groups which are not substantial enough to offset the long-term trend. Early on in the life of the 1974 Labour Government it became clear that the Chancellor was unwilling to increase child tax allowances as the Government was committed to the introduction of the child benefit scheme which entailed the phasing out of child tax allowances (CTAs). The Chancellor was likewise disposed against increasing family allowances as this was viewed as a rise in public expenditure. Instead the married man's tax allowance was raised as the way of helping families with children. But this is a very indiscriminate way of lessening the tax burden of working people with children, for half the households claiming this allowance are childless. The result of such a policy has been that the tax threshold has fallen for all groups bar one. Those whom the policy was designed most to help, families with children, saw, for example, a fall in the tax threshold as a proportion of average earnings, of 4.8 and 8.2 per cent for households with one and two children. Only for a married couple without children has their tax threshold risen. The tax threshold for a childless couple expressed as a percentage of average earnings rose by 6.9 per cent in the years since 1973/4.

Combined effects of tax changes

It is possible to show the combined effects of the changes in the vertical and horizontal incidence of direct taxation. According to available data the tax burden has increased fastest both for those on low incomes and for those households with children, compared with the childless on the same level of income. For those households on a low income who are responsible for children the tax burden has increased even faster.

The same trend can be seen from the data in Table 12.2, and particularly for those on lower incomes. For example, a single person on average earnings saw his tax burden rise by 47 per cent over the period 1964/5 to 1977/78. But the tax burden of a married couple with two children, also on average earnings, increased by 306 per cent over the same period.

A further distinction needs to be made between households with one and two earners. The best guide to the substantial changes in tax allowance relativities is to be found in Hermione Parker's work.(8) This study details the changing relative value of each of the main tax allowances.

Since 1938/9, there have been major changes in the differences in value of each of the main personal tax allowances. A single person's tax allowance has risen by 885 per cent and the married man's tax allowance by 726 per cent. The biggest change, however, has occurred in the wife's earned income relief. Before the last war it was valued at 25 per cent of the married person's tax allowance while today it has risen to 65 per cent. As a result this allowance has increased by over 2,000 per cent in the period since 1938/9. In stark contrast the child tax allowance, together with cash benefits, has risen least of all, by 189 per cent.

Here then is yet another dimension to the changing incidence of taxation in the post-war period. The poor, and families with children, have seen their tax burden increase faster than for other groups, and for poor families with children the incidence of taxation has increased even faster. But even within families with children the tax burden has not increased uniformly. The group which has lost out the most in the post-war period is low-income families with children who have only one earner.

One possible reason why the incidence of taxation has moved

horizontally against households with children, with so little public discussion, is the widespread belief that the provision of the welfare state most favours households with children. But the CSO evidence from 'The effects of taxes and benefits on households income 1976' suggests that this assumption needs to be viewed cautiously.

There are dangers in using these data to illustrate the redistributionary effect towards low income groups of the welfare state. Writing in 1968 Messrs Peacock and Shannon argued that no reliable conclusions could be drawn on the overall effect of combining tax payments and social security benefits when the analysis was based on a little over a third of government expenditure and only half of tax revenues.(9) The most recent analysis from the CSO covers 60 per cent of Government receipts and 44 per cent of all Government expenditure.(10)

Recent analysis

Since 1968 a number of studies have tried to calculate the distributionary effects of including in the analysis a higher percentage of the taxes levied and the benefits distributed in the welfare state. This work shows the allocation of the missing tax revenue and social benefits as having an important impact on the level of redistribution brought about by the welfare state. Pioneering work on this front has been carried out by J.L. Nicholson. Reporting recently, Nicholson and colleague, A.J.C. Britton, made two sets of assumptions about allocating the residual. These were that benefits of all unallocated expenditure, and the cost of unallocated taxation, fell equally on each individual, or that the net benefit from unallocated expenditure less tax fell on households in proportion to their final income. Their conclusion was that 'The extent of vertical redistribution is rather crucially dependent on the treatment of the residual.'(11)

The conclusion of Jane Peretz's work on the allocation of the residual tax and benefits in the CSO's studies is even more important to an analysis of the extent to which the overall effect of taxes and benefits favours households with children.(12) Peretz also added back a large proportion of the public expenditure which is excluded from the CSO analysis. Her findings were that 'the general effect of including these additional categories has probably been to reduce somewhat the degree of redistribution to some households which is implied. This is because these categories of expenditure are mostly on services etc used by the whole population or, in some cases, used more by the better-off'. Moreover the 'net effect of having better information about the uses of the various services could be to make a further reduction in the degree of redistribution implied.'

This conclusion needs to be borne in mind, for the main cluster of benefits which are allocated in the CSO analysis are the payment of cash allowances and the use of the main welfare state services such as schools and hospitals. Those benefits and services which are easiest to allocate in the analysis are predominantly used by families with children and by pensioners. Both Nicholson's and Peretz's work shows that to include some of the residual lessens the redistributionary effect. Peretz also suggests that to include other forms of unallocated public expenditure will lessen still further their redistributionary gains marked up to the poor and to households with children.

The belief that the welfare state redistributes generously towards families, to such an extent as to offset the increased burden of taxation amongst this group, is undermined still further by the pioneering study conducted by Muriel Nissel. *Taxes and benefits* begins by emphasising the relative increase in the burden of taxation for families with children, which has already been commented upon in this paper. Nissel then uses the CSO data to look at the redistribution bought about the welfare state. It is important to remember that Nissel is using data which have not been adjusted for the large percentage of taxes and benefits which remain unallocated and which the work of Nicholson and Britton and Peretz suggests lessens what redistribution there has been to low income groups and to families.

As well as presenting CSO data, Nissel reworks the material on the basis of adult equivalent scales, adding that these calculations are 'admittedly rough and ready but they are sufficient to bring home the point that the income available to individuals and households varies considerably at different stages of the life cycle and that it matters a great deal how many types of people live in these households'.(13)

CSO data on disposable household income after tax and benefits for a four-child family on a household basis show this group faring in 1976 very slightly better than other groups. However, once the data are reworked on an adult equivalent basis, a four-child family is shown to be slightly worse off than the average retired couple, and having only about half as much income as a non-retired couple without children. On the basis of the reworked data Nissel concludes that

'For the average household with children . . . cash benefits (including indirect benefits such as housing and food subsidies) were small and substantially outweighed by taxes'.(14)

Nissel's pioneering study shows that it is not possible to argue that the tax burden of families with children is offset by their being awarded a disproportionate share in what has become known as the social wage. In addition, we do not as yet have the reworked information along the lines of *Taxes and Benefits* to know whether the overall position of households with children has improved or deteriorated since the mid-1960s or even earlier.

Limits to redistribution

This paper has discussed three reasons for scepticism when considering the assertion that the limits of redistribution from the rich have been reached. What available data exist illustrate how limited has been the redistribution away from the top 20 or 30 per cent of the income distribution, particularly during the period since 1964. On the basis of published evidence, the carefully guarded conclusion is that there has been some redistribution from the very rich to the rich both before and after tax, but that little of the resources lost by the very rich have found their way into the pockets of the poorest 30 per cent. The Blue Book tables show the bottom 30 per cent of the income distribution commanding only 12.8 per cent of total personal incomes after tax in 1974/5.

This argues powerfully against the view that the limits of redistributing from the rich have been reached. But a second front in the campaign needs simultaneously to be opened up. The horizontal distribution of income likewise has an important effect in determining relative living standards. And this debate will entail a move away from a weekly or monthly view of income, to a lifetime's command over resources. Such a change of perspective will show the two periods of relative deprivations suffered by most households in their lifetime, whatever their level of income. Households are most vulnerable when they are responsible for children and when the breadwinners themselves move into retirement.(15)

The debate about the vertical and horizontal redistribution of resources is taking on new significance as we become more aware of the effects of moving into what might possibly prove to be a period of relatively slow economic growth. Slow growth will itself give rise to an increasing number of people made poor by unemployment, while at the same time demographic changes will increase the numbers of poor. Even if it had been substantiated that the 'limits to redistribution' had been reached, the end of economic growth marked the beginning of a new ball game for all of us.

References and Notes

1 The Political Setting

(1) Macnicol, John, *The Movement for Family Allowance, 1918–1945*, Heinemann Educational Books, 1980.
(2) Gilbert Bentley, B., *The Evolution of National Insurance in Great Britain*, Michael Joseph, 1966, chapter 2.
(3) Rathbone, Eleanor, *The Disinherited Family*, Edward Arnold, 1924.
(4) Rathbone, Eleanor, *The Case for Family Allowances*, Penguin Books, 1940, p 68.
(5) Macnicol, op cit, p 217.
(6) Land, Hilary, *The Family Wage*, University of Liverpool, 1979, p 13.
(7) Ibid.
(8) Macnicol, op cit, p 143.
(9) See Land, Hilary, 'The introduction of family allowances,' in Hall, Pheobe et al, *Change, Choice and Conflict in Social Policy*, Heinemann Educational Books, 1975, pp 211–16.
(10) See Land, Hilary, *The Family Wage*, pp 14–15, for the source of this and following quotation.
(11) Macnicol, op cit, p 145.
(12) Ibid, p 160.
(13) See Land, Hilary, op cit, pp 19–20 for this and subsequent quotations.
(14) Ibid, p 167.
(15) *Family Allowances: a memorandum by the Chancellor of the Exchequer*, Cmd 6354, 1942, p 2.
(16) *The Times*, 9 March 1945.
(17) *Hansard*, 3 November 1944, col. 1169.
(18) Macnicol, op cit, p 197.
(19) Ibid, p 94.
(20) Walley, John, *Social Security: Another British Failure*, Charles Knight, 1972, p 182.
(21) Ibid, p 182.
(22) *Social Security Bulletin*, December 1965, p. 30.
(23) *Ten Years After Beveridge*, PEP, 1952, p 25. See the author's, *Inequality in Britain*, Fontana, 1981, on how Beveridge misinterpreted these studies.
(24) Quoted in Coates, Ken and Silburn, Richard, *Poverty: the Forgotten Englishman*, Penguin, 1970, p 14.
(25) Boyd-Carpenter, John, *Way of Life*, Sidgwick and Jackson, 1980, p 137.
(26) Ibid.

(27) By the time of the 1974 Wilson Government the trade unions were using their power to influence the shape of the Government's programme in a positive way.
(28) *Hansard*, 10 November 1970, col. 253.
(29) *Diaries of a Cabinet Minister*, Hamish Hamilton and Jonathan Cape, 1976, p 443.
(30) Press release dated 12 July 1977.

2 Into Politics

(1) Marshall, T. H., *Social Policy in the Twentieth Century*, Hutchinson, 1967, p 95.
(2) *Let's go with Labour*, Labour's 1964 election manifesto.
(3) For example, the change in the National Campaign for Mental Health to MIND and the formation of new groups such as CHAR, the campaign for single homeless people.
(4) See 'An Incomes Policy for Families' in Chapter 7.
(5) Wilson, Harold, *The Labour Government 1964–1970*, Weidenfeld and Nicholson, and Michael Joseph, 1971.
(6) *Diaries of a Cabinet Minister*, Hamish Hamilton and Jonathan Cape, 1976, p 439.

Three Major Campaigns

(1) Although, of course, the Group had built up a high reputation under Lynes's stewardship and possibly it would have been able to draw on this not inconsiderable amount of goodwill to sustain the 'Poor Get Poorer' campaign.
(2) For a good introduction to the debate, see the review of W. Beckerman's *The Labour Government's Economic Policy* and the resulting correspondence in *The Listener*, 27 April–27 July 1972.
(3) *Poverty and the Labour Government*, CPAG, 1970.
(4) 22 March 1970.
(5) This and the next three quotations are from a mimeographed copy of Ennals's speech dated 19 April 1970.
(6) Letter dated 27 May 1970.
(7) Letter dated 1 June 1970.
(8) *Hansard*, 10 November 1970, col. 218–223.
(9) 'The Poverty Trap', reproduced in Chapter 7.
(10) Jones, Jack, 'Wages and social security', *New Statesman*, 7 January 1972.
(11) *Tribune*, 10 December and 24 December 1971.
(12) For a fuller account of the poverty trap debates see David Bull's essay in *Family Poverty*, ed Bull, David, second edition Duckworth, 1972.
(13) *The Castle Diaries*, Weidenfeld & Nicolson, 1980, p 737.
(14) Ibid, pp 737–8.
(15) For more details see 'Penalising All Children' (Chapter 9).
(16) Field, Frank, CPAG, 1978.

4 Pressure Group Politics

(1) *The British System of Government*, Allen & Unwin, 1967, p 105.

(2) Mackenzie, W. J. M., 'Pressure groups in British politics', reported in Rose, Richard, (ed) *Studies in British Politics*, Macmillan, 1966.

(3) Ibid, p 215.

5 The Balance Sheet

(1) *The Movement for Family Allowances*, 1918–1945, Heinemann Educational Books, 1980.

(2) *Supplementary Benefits Handbook*, HMSO, 1980, pp 40–41.

(3) Supplementary Benefits Commission, *Annual Report 1975*, Cmnd 6615, 1976, p 42.

(4) For further details on the distribution of income in the post-war world see the author's *Inequality in Britain*, Fontana, 1981, pp 22–6.

(5) *The Perception of Poverty in Europe*, Commission of the European Communities, 1977, p 71.

(6) Ibid, p 70.

6 Next Moves

(1) *Family Policy*, Michael Joseph, 1970 and Penguin Books, 1972.

(2) Atwater W. O. and Wood C. D., 'Dietary studies in New York in 1895 and 1896' in *Bulletin 46, US Department of Agriculture Office of Experimental Stations*, Washington Government Printing Office, 1898, pp 5–6.

(3) Cmnd 5116, p 3.

(4) Ibid.

(5) Ibid, p 19.

(6) This was, incidentally, the same argument put originally by the Treasury for the family allowance to be paid to fathers.

(7) Op cit, p 19.

(8) *Inequality in Britain*, Fontana, 1981, and in particular, Chapter 6.

(9) Quoted in Pond, Chris, 'Prices and prejudice', *Low Pay Bulletin*, No. 22/3, Low Pay Unit, 1978.

(10) *Inequality in Britain*.

(11) *The Movement for Family Allowances*, p 215.

(12) Ibid, p 201.

(13) Supplementary Benefits Commission, *Annual Report 1976*, Cmnd 6910, 1977, p 32.

(14) Taken from Howell, Ralph, *Why Work? A Radical Solution*, Conservative Political Centre, 1981.

(15) Field, Frank, *Fair Shares for Families: the Need for a Family Impact Statement*, Study Commission on the Family, 1980.

7 Three Political Pieces

The Poverty Trap

(1) First published in the *New Statesman*, 3 December 1971, and reproduced with the publisher's permission.

Killing a Commitment: the Cabinet *v* the Children

(1) First published in *New Society*, 17 June 1976, and reproduced with the publisher's permission.

8 The Minimum Needs of Children

(1) Simey, T. S. and M. B., *Charles Booth*, OUP, 1960, p 184.
(2) This view, which is based on the work of Professor and Mrs Simey, has not gone unchallenged. E. P. Hennock argues that the Booth Survey was not undertaken to challenge the SDF's survey — of which no copy now exists — nor was Booth surprised by his findings. For full details, see 'Poverty and Social Theory in England: the Experiences of the 1880s'. *Social History*, January 1976.
(3) Booth, C., 'The inhabitants of the Tower Hamlets (School Board Division), their condition and occupations', *JRSS*, Vol. L, 1887, p 328, (italics added).
(4) Ibid, p 178.
(5) Booth, C., 'Conditions and occupations of the people of East London and Hackney, 1887, *JRSS*, Vol. LI, 1888, p 278.
(6) Rowntree, B. S., *Poverty: A Study of Town Life*, Macmillan, 1902, p 87.
(7) Briggs, A., *Seebohm Rowntree*, Longmans, 1961, p 32.
(8) Ibid, pp 97–8.
(9) Ibid, p 98.
(10) Ibid, p 105.
(11) Ibid, p 106.
(12) Ibid.
(13) Ibid, p 108.
(14) Ibid, p 109.
(15) Bowley, A. L., *The Nature and Purpose of the Measurement of Social Phenomena*, King, 1923, pp 170–1.
(16) Rowntree, B. S., *The Human Needs of Labour*, Nelson, 1918, pp 103–4.
(17) Update from the 1906 earnings data.
(18) Beveridge, W., *Social Insurance and Allied Services*, Cmd 6404, 1942, p 14.
(19) Beveridge talked about Want instead of poverty, 'Want is one only of the five giants on the road of reconstruction . . . The others are Disease, Ignorance, Squalor and Idleness', *Social Insurance and Allied Service*, p 6.
(20) Harris, J., *William Beveridge*, Oxford, 1977, p 399.
(21) *Social Insurance and Allied Services*, p 85.
(22) Cmnd 782.
(23) Rowntree, B. S. and Lavers, G. R., *Poverty and the Welfare State*, Longmans, 1951, p 13.
(24) Plummer, V. G., *Food Values at a Glance*, Longmans, 1935, pp 45–6.
(25) Chief Medical Officer of the Ministry of Health, *Report on the State of Public Health, 1937*, HMSO, 1938, p 129.
(26) M'Gonigle, G. C. M. and Kirby, J., *Poverty and Public Health*, Gollancz, 1936, p 173.
(27) Supplementary Benefits Commission, *Low Incomes*, HMSO, 1977, p 27.
(28) Ibid, p 28.

(29) Church, M., 'Can mothers manage on supplementary benefit?' *Poverty*, No. 33, 1975, p 12.
(30) Walker, C. L. and Church, M., 'Poverty by administration', *Journal of Human Nutrition*, Vol. 32, 1978, pp 15–16.
(31) Brown, M. and Field, F., *Poor Families and Inflation*, CPAG, 1974.

9 Penalising All Children

(1) *Journal of Social Policy*, Vol. 4, Part 1, 1975.
(2) Macmillan, 1901.
(3) Thomas Nelson, 1918.
(4) Ibid, pp 87, 100–1, 103–5.
(5) *The Human Needs of Labour*, Longmans, 1937, pp 64–5, 94–101.
(6) HMSO, 1942, p 122.
(7) Ibid, pp 87–9.
(8) Wynn, M., *Family Policy*, Michael Joseph, 1970, p 55.
(9) See Field, F., Pond, C. and Meacher, M., *To Him Who Hath*, Penguin, 1977 and Field, F., *Inequality in Britain* Fontana, 1981.
(10) *The Great Child Benefit Robbery*, Child Benefit Now Campaign, 1977.
(11) For more up-to-date information see Bradshaw, Jonathan and Piachaud, David, *Child Support in the European Community*, Bedford Square Press, 1980.

10 Relating Family Income to its Needs

(1) For a different interpretation and one with which I am now in agreement see Macnicol, John, *The Movement for Family Allowances*, 1918–1945, Heinemann Educational Books, 1980.
(2) Quoted in Land, H., 'The Introduction of Family Allowances' Hall, P. et al, *Change, Choice and Conflict in Social Policy*, Heinemann Educational Books, 1975, p 224.
(3) Rathbone, Eleanor, *The Disinherited Family*, Edward Arnold, 1924.
(4) Rathbone, Eleanor, *Family Allowances*, Allen & Unwin, 1949, p 21.
(5) Ibid, p 25.
(6) Walley, John, *Social Security: Another British Failure*, Charles Knight, 1972, p 84.
(7) Ibid, p 182.
(8) Ibid.
(9) Ibid, p 183.
(10) *The Great Child Benefit Robbery*, Child Benefit Now Campaign, 1977, p 8.
(11) Ministry of Social Security, *Circumstances of Families*, HMSO, 1967.
(12) See 'Killing a Commitment', reproduced in Chapter 7, for fuller details.
(13) Renamed 'one-parent benefit' in 1981.
(14) An example of how this charge was made see the author's *All Children Worse off under Labour*, CPAG, 1978.
(15) *Poverty: A Study of Town Life*, Macmillan, 1902 edition, p 136.
(16) Atkinson, A. B., 'Low Pay and the Cycle of Poverty' in *Low Pay*, ed Field, F., Arrow, 1973, p 109.

11 Poverty, Growth and the Redistribution of Income

(1) Ennals, D., DHSS press release dated 19 April 1970.
(2) Fiegehan, G. C., Lansley, P. S. and Smith, A. D., *Poverty and Progress in Britain 1953–73*, CUP, 1977, p 29.
(3) Ibid, p 29.
(4) Ibid.
(5) Ibid.
(6) Royal Commission on the Distribution of Income and Wealth, *Lower Incomes*, HMSO, 1978, p 18.
(7) Ibid.
(8) See Chapter 8 for further details.
(9) For further details, see Field, F., 'Low pay, low profile', *Low Pay Bulletin*, No. 18, 1977.
(10) Atkinson, A. B., 'Low pay and the cycle of poverty' in *Low Pay*, ed. Field, F., Arrow, 1973, pp 116–7.
(11) Royal Commission on the Distribution of Income and Wealth, op cit.
(12) 'New projections of future labour force', *DE Gazette*, June 1977.
(13) Beveridge, W., *Social Insurance and Allied Services*, HMSO, 1942, para 20.
(14) Nevertheless the number of pensioners over 75 is expected to grow significantly and this trend will have important repercussions on the cost of social service provision.
(15) See Chapter 12 for the development of this theme.

12 Limits to Redistribution:
What Limits and What Kind of Redistribution?

(1) Crosland, C. A. R., *A Social Democratic Britain*, Fabian Society, 1971, pp 2–3.
(2) See Chapter 11.
(3) Royal Commission on the Distribution of Income and Wealth, Report No. 1, *Initial Report on the Standing Reference*, Cmnd 6171, HMSO, 1975, pp 37–8.
(4) Ibid, pp 43–4.
(5) Field, F., Pond, C. and Meacher, M., *To Him Who Hath*, Penguin Books, 1977.
(6) Willis, J. R. M. and Hardwick, P. T. W., *Tax Expenditure in the UK*, Heinemann Educational Books, 1978, p 89.
(7) Ibid, p 15.
(8) Parker, Hermione, *Who Pays for the Children?*, Outer Circle Policy Unit, 1978.
(9) Peacock, A. and Shannon, R., 'The welfare state and the redistribution of income', *Westminister Bank Review*, August, 1968.
(10) Stephenson, G. A., 'The effect of taxes and benefits on household income, 1976', *Economic Trends*, February, 1978.
(11) Nicholson, J. L. and Britton, A. J. C., 'The redistribution of income' in Atkinson, A. B., (ed), *The Personal Distribution of Incomes*, Allen & Unwin, 1976.
(12) Peretz, J., 'Beneficiaries of public expenditure: an analysis for 1971/1972', mimeograph n d.

(13) Nissel, M., *Taxes and Benefits: Does Redistribution Help the Family?*, Policy Studies Institute, 1978, p 3.
(14) Ibid, p 4.
(15) Field, F., *Priority for Children*, Child Poverty Action Group, 1978.

Index